Top 25 locator map
(continues on inside
back cover)

◄──────

C000163696

CityPack
Singapore

VIVIEN LYTTON

If you have any comments
or suggestions for this guide
you can contact the editor at
Citypack@theAA.com

AA Publishing
Find out more about AA Publishing and the wide
range of services the AA provides by visiting our
website at *www.theAA.com/bookshop*

About This Book

ORGANIZATION

This guide is divided into six chapters:
- Planning Ahead, Getting There
- Living Singapore—Singapore Now, Singapore Then, Time to Shop, Out and About, Walks, Singapore by Night
- Singapore's Top 25 Sights
- Singapore's Best—best of the rest
- Where To—detailed listings of restaurants, hotels, shops and nightlife
- Travel Facts—practical information

In addition, easy-to-read side panels provide extra facts and snippets, highlights of places to visit and invaluable practical advice.

The colors of the tabs on the page corners match the colors of the triangles aligned with the chapter names on the contents page opposite.

MAPS

The fold-out map in the wallet at the back of this book is a comprehensive street plan of Singapore. The first (or only) grid reference given for each attraction refers to this map. **The Top 25 locator map** found on the inside front and back covers of the book itself is for quick reference. It shows the Top 25 Sights, described on pages 26–50, which are clearly plotted by number (**1**–**25**, not page number) across the city. The second map reference given for the Top 25 Sights refers to this map.

Contents

Planning Ahead

WHEN TO GO

The best time to visit Singapore is around Chinese New Year, although you will need to book a hotel well in advance. July is sale time in Orchard Road, so shoppers take note. Otherwise, the city hums along year-round, catering to holiday and business travelers alike with many festivals and events on offer.

TIME

Singapore is eight hours ahead of GMT, 13 hours ahead of New York, and two hours behind Sydney.

AVERAGE DAILY MAXIMUM TEMPERATURES

JAN	FEB	MAR	APR	MAY	JUN	JUL	AUG	SEP	OCT	NOV	DEC
86°F	88°F	88°F	89°F	90°F	90°F	87°F	88°F	88°F	88°F	88°F	86°F
30°C	31°C	31°C	32°C	32°C	32°C	31°C	31°C	31°C	31°C	31°C	30°C

WEATHER Singapore's climate is tropical, with very few seasonal variations. The temperature range is steady, from a night-time low of 24°C (75°F) to a daily high of 31°C (88°F). December and January can be slightly cooler and May to August slightly hotter. Rainfall peaks between November and January, with the northeast monsoon. However, it rarely rains for long—usually an hour's torrential downpour at a time. During monsoon times, storms can be dramatic, with sheets of rain and intense thunder and lightning. Most occur early in the morning and in the afternoon. Humidity can sometimes reach nearly 100 percent, and averages 84 percent.

WHAT'S ON

January *River Raft Race*: All manner of rafts race on the Singapore River, plus bands, cheerleaders and food stalls. *Thaipusam*: This Hindu festival displays dramatic feats of mind over matter.
January/February *Chinese New Year*: A two-day public holiday, with fireworks, stalls and dragon dances.
February *Chingay Procession*: A huge street carnival based on a Chinese folk festival. Lion dancers, acrobats, bands and floats.
March *Singapore Food Festival*.

April *Singapore International Film Festival*
June *Dragon Boat Festival*: 20 teams enter this longboat race.
Singapore Arts Festival: One of Asia's leading contemporary arts festivals.
July *Great Singapore Sale*: Orchard Road hosts this price-cutting month around July, to highlight Singapore as a major shopping destination.
August *National Day*: 9 August. This public holiday marks Singapore's independence from the British.

August/September *Festival of the Hungry Ghosts*: Fun and feasting.
September *Mooncake Festival*: A colorful spectacle named after the delicious mooncakes on sale.
October *Thimithi*: Fire-walking ceremony.
October/November *Festival of the Nine Emperor Gods*: A week of processions and street opera.
November *Deepavali*: Lamps are lit to celebrate the triumph of good over evil.
December *Christmas*: Orchard Road lights up.

SINGAPORE ONLINE

Not surprisingly for such a small island nation, Singapore has been fully wired for broadband and has embraced the global digital culture.

www.visitsingapore.com

This dynamic site, with special sections for US and UK visitors, has up-to-date details of events, exhibitions, holiday ideas and accommodations suggestions. For serious shoppers there is a list of errant retailers.

www.asia1.com.sg

Singapore's main media group's portal. Links to all major national print media websites, plus regional news.

www.tourismsingapore.com

The Singapore Tourism Board's comprehensive guide for pre-travel planning. Includes trip planner, attraction reviews, travel package details and advice on where best to stay.

www.sg.yahoo.com

Comprehensive local portal with news, links to entertainment, arts, media, education and sports websites, and business news.

www.singapore.tourism-asia.com

Plenty of up-to-date information on this site, with good sections on general travel, attractions, shopping and entertainment.

www.asiatravelmart.com

Asia's major online travel marketplace with various hotel and flight booking information, plus booking forms.

www.straitstimes.asia1.com.sg

Singapore's major daily newspaper's website with local and international news, commentary, forums and business news.

www.thingstodo-singapore.com.sg

A good site to research your Singapore trip. Includes dining, entertainment, shopping and attraction information.

GOOD TRAVEL SITES

www.fodors.com

A complete travel-planning site. You can research prices and weather; book air tickets, cars and rooms; ask questions (and get answers) from fellow travelers; and find links to other sites.

www.changi.airport.com.sg

Features arrival and departure details, airport facilities, and shopping and dining information in both terminals.

CYBERCAFÉS

Chills Café

➕ E6 ✉ 01–07, 39 Stamford Road ☎ 6883 1016 🕐 Daily 9.30am–midnight 💵 S$5 per hour

Surf@Café

➕ D6 ✉ 277 Orchard Road ☎ 6737 4901 🕐 9.30am–11.30pm 💵 S$6 per hour

Cybernet Cafe

➕ Off map ✉ Level 3, Terminal 2, Changi Airport ☎ 6546 1968 🕐 7am–11pm 💵 S$8 per hour

Getting There

INSURANCE

Check your insurance policy and purchase supplementary cover if necessary. Make sure you are covered for medical expenses.

MONEY

The unit of currency is the Singapore dollar. Brunei dollar notes have the same value as the Singapore dollar and are accepted everywhere in Singapore. The Singapore dollar and other major currencies are easily changed to local currency in Malaysia and Indonesia. Traveler's checks are readily accepted.

$10

$50

$100

$1000

ARRIVING

Singapore's Changi Airport is 12 miles (20km) east of the city center and is well served by flights from major destinations. Flights take around 13 hours from Western Europe and around 20 hours from the US. The huge airport has two terminals, many lounges and hundreds of shops.

ARRIVING AT CHANGI AIRPORT

For airport inquiries ☎ 6542 1122; www. changi airport.com.sg. For customs information ► 88. Take the MRT train connection for easy access to all parts of the island. You can go to Tanaj Merah station and switch to the westbound train service to be in the city in less than 30 minutes; the fare is S$1.40. Inquires ☎ 1800 336 8900.
Taxi ranks are well marked and there is rarely a line. The fare into the city is around S$25.
The Airbus (☎ 6542 8297) stops at major hotels in the city (journey time 30 minutes; cost S$7). It runs from 6am to midnight and can be picked up from just outside the terminal.
Public buses 16 and 38 also travel to the city (6am to midnight, journey time 50 minutes; cost S$2). Pick them up below terminals 1 and 2.

ARRIVING BY BUS

Air-conditioned long-distance buses come direct from Bangkok, Penang and Kuala Lumpur, and from other main towns in peninsular Malaysia. Singapore–Kuala Lumpur Express (☎ 6292 8254; www.supercoach.com.sg; journey time 6 hours; cost S$20). For Penang the

Pan Malaysian Express (☎ 6294 7034; www.impression.com.sg; journey time 12–14 hours; cost S$30). Fares to Bangkok are S$70 for the 20–24 hour journey (☎ 6294 5415) with buses from the Golden Mile Complex in Beach Road. Long-distance buses from Malaysia arrive and depart from the Lavender Street bus station.

Bus 170 leaves the bus station at Johor Bahru (the Malaysian city visible across the causeway from Singapore) regularly for Ban San bus station in Singapore (Singapore–Johor Bahru Express ☎ 6292 8149; journey time one hour; cost S$1.70). The Second Crossing, another causeway, links Tuas in Singapore's west with Malaysia's Johor state. All bus travelers break their journeys for immigration formalities.

ARRIVING BY TRAIN

There is one main north-south train line in Malaysia. Around three trains arrive per day in Singapore from Kuala Lumpur. Journey times vary but average 6 hours (for KTM timetables check www.ktmb.com.my). Immigration formalities occur once you have disembarked at Singapore's Keppel Road railway station, still technically in Malaysia (☎ 6222 5165). The Eastern and Oriental Express offers a leisurely and luxurious trip to Singapore from Bangkok, Penang or Kuala Lumpur (☎ 6392 3500).

ARRIVING BY SEA

Most cruise ships dock at the World Trade Centre. From there, taxis and buses go to central Singapore. Ferries travel regularly between Tanjong Belungkor (Johor) and Changi ferry terminal (Ferrylink ☎ 6545 3600; journey time 45 minutes; cost S$20); to and from Tioman March to October (Auto Batam Ferries ☎ 6542 7102; journey time 4 hours 30 minutes; cost S$106); and between the World Trade Centre and Bintan (Auto Batam Ferries ☎ 6271 4866; journey time 1 hour 30 minutes; cost S$40).

GETTING AROUND

Public transportation in Singapore is very good and consists of buses, the MRT and taxis. For information ► 90–91.

Living
Singapore

Singapore Now

Above: *Worshippers' shoes outside a temple*

Singapore, relatively small as world capitals go, is a dramatic artifact of colonial and modern times. A planner's dream, the city has first-class transportation and communication systems, flashy hotels and glitzy shopping malls, and one of the world's great airports. Tree-lined avenues, landscaped urban areas, small parks and roadside tropical greenery are commonplace. It is the envy of many cities for its orderliness and civil obedience. Singapore's economic potency as a manufacturing and shipping hub, and as

NEIGHBORHOODS

• Singapore's near-city neighborhoods—each one with a distinct character based on its ethnic or colonial origins—are within easy reach by bus or MRT (Mass Rapid Transit). South of the river, Chinatown comes alive at festival time and the back streets have great antique shops and just to the north is the CBD (Central Business District), with its tall office towers; across the river, the colonial district is set around the Padang, several museums and Raffles Hotel. Heading westward, busy Orchard Road is an international retail hub and along Serangoon Road, to the north, Indian culture thrives. Nearby Kampung Glam, once the home to the Sultan of Singapore, has long been at the heart of Malay culture. But try to discover some more out-of-the-way places, such as the central nature reserve of Bukit Timah, delightful Pulau Ubin, on the northeast of the island, or any one of the masses of public housing precincts where Singaporeans live.

A FINE CITY

• You may have heard that Singapore is a fine city (you can even buy the T-shirt). The government's perfectly reasonable campaign to keep the city clean, and its citizens socially responsible, has led to it imposing fines of up to $1,000 for such acts as littering, jaywalking or even failure to flush a public lavatory. However, possession of chewing gum has recently been taken off the list of banned activities.

Above: *Music played outside the rebuilt Chettiar Temple*

Asia's premier financial center, are constantly being strengthened by a government keen to bring new technology and research industries to an island that makes its way forward with only human resources as its base. Every aspect of life in Singapore is carefully controlled and monitored by a government concerned to maintain the city state's high growth rates. But there are signs that local constructive criticism, once officially suppressed, or at least discouraged, is again flourishing due to a somewhat more benign government policy.

Most of Singapore's predominantly Chinese population, three-quarters of the city's inhabitants, arrived three or four generations ago from provinces in southern China and nearby Malacca. Malays make up the next largest sector of the population and Indians less than a tenth. There are also numerous Eurasians and expatriate workers from all over the world, a result of Singapore's colonial and trading history and importance today as a regional capital. This diversity of races, religions and creeds, exemplified by Singapore's many festivals and traditions, make the city a most bright and

11

Above: *Hundreds of Hindu deities look down from the Sri Mariamman Temple*
Above right: *A rickshaw driver takes a well-earned break*

vibrant destination. And have you ever wondered how Singapore grew so quickly? Take a bus trip along Serangoon Road on Saturday or Sunday evenings and you'll see thousands of Sri Lankan, Bangladeshi and other foreign nationals crowding the streets, socializing and enjoying their time off. The island state has about 300,000 foreign workers employed under one of the strictest guest worker programs in the world. The construction industry can hire four foreigners for every Singaporean employee, and working and living conditions (not to mention pay) differ greatly from those that the locals enjoy. A worker generally stays for two years and occupational health and safety rules are regularly ignored. And more than 100,000 domestic workers, mostly from the Philippines, Indonesia, Sri

ISLANDS AROUND THE ISLAND

• Singapore's best known island is the recreational Sentosa, once a British fort. But the country is surrounded by over 50 small islands, although they're pretty much occupied by the military, oil refineries or nature reserves. In the south, St John's Island is a popular picnic destination, while Kusu Island has a turtle sanctuary.

Lanka and Burma, are employed by middle-class working couples. On Sundays, they leave work behind them and meet friends to enjoy their day off in the parks and malls along Orchard Road.

Despite the island's impressive development in the last 50 years, seen in the cityscape of tower blocks, freeways and glitzy shopping malls, pockets of old Singapore remain. Visit some of the backstreets of Chinatown, with its prosperous traders; stroll around Little India and chance upon fortunetellers giving pavement consultation; or trawl for delicious foodstuffs at dusk around the mosques during Ramadan and you'll realize a different Singapore exists. You

Above: *Reaching up to Singapore's skyline*

SINGLISH

• You're bound to come across Singlish, the local colloquial English, if you get talking to many Singaporeans. You'll know someone is speaking Singlish if they throw the word lah in at every opportunity to show emphasis. Other examples include: *fli-end* (friend), *tok kong* (very good) and *lerf* (love). Of course, Singlish is officially frowned upon by a government eager to ensure high standards of verbal communication.

GOING REGIONAL

• With such a small land size, Singapore is expanding its economic base to China, where it has developed an industrial township near Shanghai, and India, where a Singapore consortium has built a technology park at Bangalore. There are other developments in Vietnam, Thailand and Indonesia.

Above: *Practising tai-chi in the park*
Above right: *Strolling through an underpass alongside the Singapore River*

might like to soak up the atmosphere of Raffles Hotel—with a gin and tonic in hand, of course— and imagine the island's colonial history when it was one of Britain's prized Crown Colonies. And the small oases of undeveloped tropical rain-forest at Bukit Timah, as well as coastal mangrove remnants, provide an idea of the natural environment that once covered the island. Massive land reclamation has consider-ably extended the island state—it's difficult to believe as you gaze seaward toward the hundreds of new buildings that extend to the classy Marina area, with its new theater complex, that Raffles Hotel was once a water-front building.

SINGAPORE RIVER

• In recent years, ambitious projects to develop the banks of the Singapore River as dining and entertainment areas have drawn visitors back to the river's edge. After decades of being a backwater following the development of the modern port areas and CBD, the riverbank is once again bustling. The carefully restored and re-created shophouses and warehouses along Boat Quay, Clarke Quay and the upper river now offer a wide selection of popular theme restaurants and shops, tempting tourists, expatriates and locals.

Above: *At the Dragon Dance*

The Singapore River bisects the center of the city, with the core of the original colonial government buildings and the Padang, the colonial village green, on the north bank and remnants of the old areas originally settled by Indian, Arab and Malay inhabitants beyond. Outside the central city core are the extensive residential and industrial areas, in particular a number of huge "new town" estates—block upon block of medium- and high-rise apartment buildings. All these towns are self-sufficient, offering good shopping, recreational and educational facilities, and most are linked to the city by an efficient Mass Rapid Transit (MRT) system. Originally developed as public housing, the majority of apartment dwellings are now privately owned.

With its close location to the equator and an average humidity often above 90 percent, the island's tropical climate can sap the energies of the most ardent traveler. Fortunately air-conditioning rules in Singapore—shops, hotels and public transportation are all climate controlled. So board a bus, ride the MRT or hail a cab and explore the delights of this cosmopolitan island state.

SINGAPORE IN FIGURES

- Religions: Taoist/ Buddhist 54 percent; Muslims 15 percent; Christian 13 percent; Hindu 4 percent; other/none 14 percent.

- Population in 1819 500; population in 2002 3.5 million.

- Per capita income in 1965 US$300; in 2000 US$27,740.

- Singapore is 62 miles (100km) from the equator).

15

Singapore Then

Above from the left: *Hallway Raffles Hotel; Raffles Hotel; Sam Po Kong Temple; Singapore Botanic Gardens*

EARLY DAYS

The first mention of Singapore comes in Chinese seafaring records of the 3rd century AD, where it is referred to as "Pu lou Chung" (island at the end of the peninsula). In the late 13th century Marco Polo noted a thriving city, possibly a satellite of the flourishing Sumatran Srivijayan empire. It could have been Singapore, then called Temasek. *Sejarah Melayu* (Malay annals of the 16th century) note a 13th-century Singapura (Lion City).

In the late 14th century, the island's ruler, Parameswara, fled to Melaka. For 400 years Singapore was all but abandoned except for visiting pirates and fishermen.

1819 British official Thomas Raffles selects Singapore as a trading post between China and India. It is also near to newly acquired British colonies.

1826 With Penang and Melaka, Singapore becomes part of the British-run Straits Settlements.

1867 Singapore is designated a Crown Colony under British rule. It becomes a hub of international trade.

1870s Thousands of immigrants from south China begin arriving in Singapore. They work in shipyards and rubber plantations, and as small traders.

1887 Henry Ridley, director of the Botanic Gardens, propagates Asia's first rubber trees. Raffles Hotel opens.

1921 Japan's increasing military might causes the British to start building coastal defenses.

1942 Singapore falls to the Japanese.

1945 British Lord Louis Mountbatten accepts the Japanese surrender.

1954 Singapore's first elections: a legislative council is elected to advise the governor. Lee Kuan Yew helps found the People's Action Party (PAP).

1955 A Legislative Assembly is set up. David Marshall becomes Singapore's first chief minister.

1957 Malaya becomes independent. Singapore is a separate colony.

1959 PAP forms Singapore's first government. Lee Kuan Yew is appointed prime minister.

1963 Singapore forms the Federation of Malaysia with Malaya, Sarawak and North Borneo.

1965 Singapore leaves the Federation and becomes an independent republic.

1966 The Singapore dollar becomes the official currency.

1968 The British announce military withdrawal.

1977 2,913 acres (1,179ha) of land is reclaimed from the sea.

1990 Lee Kuan Yew steps aside, into the newly created post of senior minister.

2000 Singapore recovers from the Asian economic crisis.

2004 Government works to keep the SARS epidemic under control.

JAPANESE OCCUPATION

In 1942 the Japanese launched their attack on Singapore. Despite being outnumbered three to one, they gained control of the colony in just a few days, during which time tens of thousands of British, Indian and Australian troops were killed or wounded. During the occupation up to 50,000 Chinese men were executed and the Allied troops were interned or dispatched to work on the infamous "Death" railway.

LEE KUAN YEW

Lee Kuan Yew is credited with transforming Singapore from a Third World trading port to a highly developed nation. Known for hard work and discipline, he encouraged developments in housing, education, infrastructure and manufacture, with amazing results.

17

Time to Shop

Shopping in Singapore is a very serious activity. Without a doubt, the city is Southeast Asia's shopping capital and shops seem to outnumber its inhabitants. Singapore's Orchard Road (➤ 32,

SALE TIME

Visitors from late May to mid-July should take advantage of the Great Singapore Sale. There's hardly a store on the island that doesn't participate in this stock-moving exercise, when goods of all descriptions are marked down. The sale even has its own website with store coupons and cash prizes at www.greatsingaporesale.com.sg.

72–73) provides a comprehensive shopping experience equal to other world capitals and is particularly recommended for brand-name fashion goods, electronics and cameras. But the benefit of Singapore shopping to those interested in ethnic souvenirs or Asian antiques is that the nation state's racial mix of Chinese, Malay and Indian means that all types of goods from these cultures can be found in the specialist shops, especially those for sale in the different ethnic quarters of the city. From the Chinese neighborhood you will find porcelain, masks, silk and traditional paintings; from the Malay there's basketware, Ikat cloth, batiks, puppets, sarongs and leatherware; and from the Indian quarter paintings, jewelry, scupltures and pottery.

Not surprisingly, given Singapore's hot and humid weather, every large building has air-conditioning. Major department stores include Tangs, Robinsons and Takashimaya. Be sure to check out Far East Plaza in Scotts Road for younger fashions. For small, inexpensive souvenirs, take the MRT to Bugis. For cameras and electronic equipment try Lucky Plaza and Sim Lim Square, armed with your STB good retailers guide (➤ side bar) and the Funan IT Mall

Below: *Dragon mask, Chinatown*
Below left: *Take your pick of Malaysian chilis*

on North Bridge Road. The huge Marina Square, including Millenia Walk, five minutes' walk from Raffles City MRT station, has lots of homeware shops. Chinatown has a mix of souvenir and antique shops including the very interesting People's Park Complex—still popular with locals—a good example of Singapore retailing circa the 1960s. In the colonial district try the lovely CHIJMES mall and nearby Raffles City for fashion and food. Antique lovers should check out Tanglin Mall and the Paragon Shopping Centre. While bargaining in the markets and suburban shops is considered part of the Singapore experience, and most electronic stores and jewelers will allow you to haggle a little, brand-name boutiques and department stores throughout Singapore have fixed and clearly marked prices.

Finally, the Sunday flea markets at Clarke Quay and the incredible Thieves' Market at Sungei Road are a chance to pick up a bargain and to see yet another side of Singapore's retail scene.

CONSUMER PROTECTION

Since Singaporeans and the 6 million annual visitors to the island take shopping seriously, the Singapore government is very keen to promote hassle-free, safe shopping for consumers. To aid and protect shoppers the Singapore Tourism Board (STB) publishes a shopping guide (available at tourism offices) which lists good retailers—those preferred retailers chosen for their service and reliability—and a list of retailers to avoid. A special hotline number, 1800 736 3366, has been set up to assist tourists who have had bad retail experiences during their stay in Singapore.

Out and About

CONTACT DETAILS

STB
✉ Tourism Court, 1
Orchard Spring Lane
☎ 1800 736 2000
🕐 Mon–Fri 8.30–5; Sat
8.30–1

Singapore Trolley Bus
🕐 Buses start at the
Botanic Gardens at 9.45,
10.15, 2.45, 3.15 ☎ 6339
6833

Trishaw Tours Pte Ltd
☎ 6545 6311 ❓ Agree
on the price before starting

**Singapore River Cruises
and Leisure**
☎ 6336 6111 🚢 From
Empress Place and the
middle of Boat Quay

WaterTours
☎ 6533 9811
🚢 Harbor trips at 10.30,
3 and 6.30, departing
from Clifford Pier

INFORMATION

**CHANGI PRISON
CHAPEL AND MUSEUM**
Distance 14 miles (22km)
Journey Time 1 hour
✉ Upper Changi Road,
Changi Village
☎ 6543 0893
🕐 Mon–Sat 10–5
🚇 MRT to Tanah Merah
then bus 2
🍴 Changi Village is a
good place for lunch

ORGANIZED SIGHTSEEING

Tours are generally by air-conditioned long-distance bus. Various trips are available, including trips to individual attractions, such as Singapore Zoo; city and island tours; history tours focusing on Raffles, the colonial era, the Civic

District and World War II; and shopping and horse-racing trips. Be aware that tours cost considerably more than going to the same places on you own. The Singapore Trolley Bus plies between some of the city's major attractions. One-day tickets for unlimited travel are available. For comprehensive tour information, contact the Singapore Tourism Board (STB). The *Singapore Official Guide* lists most tours and is free, as are *Singapore This Week* and *The Singapore Visitor*.

EXCURSIONS
CHANGI PRISON CHAPEL AND MUSEUM

During World War II, some 85,000 civilians, Allied troops and prisoners were incarcerated. Exhibits at the Changi Prison Chapel and Museum portray the terrible conditions they endured—some for more than three years. Located on the grounds of the current prison, the chapel is a reconstruction of the small, open-air structure built by prisoners of war. Some prisoners managed to record their experiences of Changi, none more movingly than W. R. M. Haxworth, whose sketches vividly capture his years in Changi. George Aspinall, then only 17, secretly photographed life in the prison.

JOHOR BAHRU

The Malaysian city of Johor Bahru (JB, as it is popularly known) is a marked contrast to the 'clean and green' Lion City. The Istana Besar, with its beautiful gardens and Royal Museum, and the Sultan Abu Bakar Mosque are worth visiting. Both

are located off Jalan Tun Dr Ismail and Both were built by Sultan Abu Bakar, in 1866 and 1900 respectively. Abu Bakar loved all things English and the furniture is reminiscent of what you might find in a British stately home. JB is famed for its seafood and at weekends many Singaporeans cross the causeway. Advantageous exchange rates have made the city big for shopping. Dollars can be changed to ringgit at banks or exchange bureaus in JB and Singapore.

SUNGEI BULOH NATURE RESERVE

Singapore's only wetland nature reserve covers 88ha. Carefully planned walkways allow you to explore brackish swamps, mangrove and mudflat habitats, and to observe tropical birdlife and many species of marine creatures, particularly mudskippers and crabs. Early morning and evening are the best times for viewing wildlife, with birdlife most evident before 10AM. From September to March, the reserve is home to migratory birds from as far afield as eastern Siberia. An audio-visual show is screened in the exhibition hall five times a day at 9am, 11am, 1pm, 3pm and 5pm.

Below far left: *Monkey in Singapore Zoo*
Below: *The Victorian palace of Istana Besar*

INFORMATION

JOHOR BAHRU
Distance 17 miles (27km)
Journey Time 1 hour
🚌 From Queen Street. Go through customs on foot and rejoin any onward 170
❓ Not everything on sale in Malaysia can be legally brought into Singapore, including pirated videos and software

JOHOR BAHRU ROYAL MUSEUM
✉ Jalan Tun Dr. Ismail, 15 minutes' walk west of the border
☎ 02 07 223 0555
🕐 Sat–Thu 9–4
💰 Expensive

INFORMATION

SUNGEI BULOH NATURE RESERVE
Distance 15 miles (24km)
Journey Time 1 hour
✉ Off Neo Tiew Crescent
☎ 6794 1401
🕐 Mon–Fri 7.30–7; Sat, Sun and public hols 7–7
🚇 Woodlands or Kranji then TIBS bus 925 to Kranji reservoir parking lot and walk 15–20 minutes. On Sundays the 925 goes the entire way

21

Walks

INFORMATION

Morning
Distance 3 miles (5km)
Time 3 hours
Start point Maxwell Road hawker center
➕ blll; E8
🚇 Tanjong Pagar
End point Boat Quay
➕ dl; E7
🚇 Raffles Place

Afternoon
Distance 3 miles (5km)
Time 3 hours
Start point Boat Quay
➕ dl; E7
🚇 Raffles Place
End point Victoria Street
➕ F6
🚇 Bugis

Evening
Distance 2 miles (3km)
Time 1 hour
Start and end point Serangoon Road
➕ E5
🚇 Bugis

AROUND SINGAPORE'S HISTORIC CORE

Allow a full day for this walk, with breaks for meals, or choose part of it for a shorter walk.

Morning For an all-day walk, start as early as possible with coffee at Maxwell Road hawker center. Walk down South Bridge Road to Smith Street on your left; take this street and return to South Bridge Road via Trengganu, Temple and Pagoda streets (► 28). Notice the renovated Chinese shophouses (ground-floor shops with dwellings above) and visit Singapore's oldest Hindu temple, the Sri Mariamman Temple (► 42). Cross over and take Ann Siang Hill, then turn left down Club Street. Turn right at Cross Street and left into Telok Ayer Street. Fuk Tak Ch'i Temple now houses a museum, while Far East Square and China Square are full of places to eat. Turn right down Cheang Hong Lim Street and then left at the end. Follow Cecil Street and D'Almeida Street into Raffles Place. Continue straight into Bonham Street and left into Boat Quay (► 38). Have lunch at one of the many restaurants there.

Afternoon Walk along the riverbank until you come to Cavenagh Bridge. Cross over and pass Empress Place and the Victoria Concert Hall and Theatre. On your right is the Singapore Cricket Club (members only are admitted).

Cross over High Street and take St. Andrew's Road, passing the Supreme Court, City Hall and St. Andrew's Cathedral on your left. The Padang is on your right. After Raffles City you come to Raffles Hotel (► 26)—an ideal place for afternoon tea. Try Ah Teng's Bakery (► 71) or the Seah Street Deli (you can walk through the hotel and its shopping arcade to reach these cafés). Continue along Beach Road. Turn left into Arab Street, right into Baghdad Street and left into Bussorah Street. Sultan Mosque (► 47), at the end of this street, is magnificent. Facing the

mosque, take the side street to your left and then head right up Arab Street to the intersection with Victoria Street. Wander around a number of streets lined with old shops selling cloth and handicrafts. You'll probably need a break and a shower back at your hotel.

Above: Take a walk down Arab Street

Evening Take in Little India (► 29), starting at the beginning of Serangoon Road with the market on your left and the Little India Arcade on the right. Try side-street detours (including a left up Buffalo Road, then a right into Race Course Road, to find the banana-leaf restaurants, where food is served on banana leaves (► 65) and then walk to Serangoon Plaza. Walk back down the other side of Serangoon Road, enjoying the bustling side streets. You'll be tempted for dinner long before you reach the start of Serangoon Road—guaranteed.

Far left: Sultan Ahmad Shah mosque

Below: Tasty treats of satay and accompaniments

Singapore by Night

Above: *Visions of the night*

DRINK PRICES

To get the night off to a good start, and compensate for Singapore's generally high drink prices, take advantage of the happy hours that run from around 5–8pm. Also, many places offer cheap or free drinks for women–check with bars and clubs beforehand (➤ 82, 83).

WHAT'S ON

Look in the mainstream media such as the *Straits Times* and *Eight Days* (weekly entertainment magazine), pick up the free entertainment magazines such as *I-S Magazine* and *Where Singapore*, or log on to www.asiabynight.com/singapore. Tickets for live performances can be purchased from www.sistic.com.sg

STEPPING OUT

Singapore is one of the world's great night cities. Retail stores remain open until 9 or 10pm daily, hawker food stands–with their incomparable aromas wafting through the streets–and restaurants provide fantastic choices of cuisine, and bars and clubs are often still packed into the early hours, particularly on Friday and Saturday nights. Main areas to head for include Orchard Road (especially Emerald Hill); Boat, Robertson and Clarke quays; Chinatown (Far East Square district); and the Colonial District (CHIJMES). Around Bugis Street there's always some action, although the area is not as risqué as it was in times past, when it was the city's transsexual meeting place. If you are looking to mix with expats, try Holland Village or the Orchard Road hotels. Finally, you're perfectly safe wherever you go, since assualts on tourists are virtually unheard of in Singapore.

RIVERSIDE ACTION

Arguably the best choice for those new to town is to head for Boat Quay (➤ 38) or Clarke Quay/Riverside Point (➤ 40) districts. Both areas have extensive pedestrian walkways, lots of bars, clubs and restaurants to choose from, and a riverside nightlife ambience that is typically Singaporean. Alternatively, take an evening river cruise to get a different perspective of this vibrant city with its contrasting old and new architecture and the night lights. Or head for one of the city's many dance clubs (➤ 83) for live or house music and a chance to party with the locals.

SINGAPORE's
top 25 sights

The sights are shown on the maps on the inside front cover and inside back cover, numbered **1**–**25** across the city

Raffles Hotel

HIGHLIGHTS

- Front façade
- Lobby
- Tiffin Room
- Bar and Billiard Room
- Singapore Sling
- Raffles Hotel Museum
- Palm Court
- Long Bar

INFORMATION

www.raffleshotel.com
- ✚ F6
- ✉ 1 Beach Road
- ☎ 6337 1886
- 🍴 Two cafés, bakery, Chinese restaurant, grill, tiffin room, deli and "fusion" restaurant
- 🚇 City Hall
- 🚌 14, 16, 36, 56, 82, 100, 107, 125, 167
- ♿ Good
- ↔ Fort Canning Park (➤ 36), the Padang (➤ 37), Boat Quay (➤ 38)
- ❔ Free museum 🕐 Daily 10–7; shopping arcade

The renovators may have tried too hard—the Long Bar, for instance, was repositioned to allow for a two-story bar to cater to the hordes of visitors—but Raffles remains the Grand Old Lady of the East.

Legend Say "Raffles" and you conjure up an image of the very epitome of colonial style and service. Established by the Sarkies brothers in 1887, the hotel served the traders and travelers who, after the opening of the Suez Canal in 1869, were visiting the bustling commercial hub of Singapore in growing numbers. Within just a decade of opening, the original 10-room bungalow had been expanded and the two-story wings added. The main building, the front part, was opened in 1899. Over the years the Raffles Hotel has acquired a worldwide reputation for fine service and food, with its charming blend of classical architecture and tropical gardens. The elegant Raffles Courtyard is at the back of the main building.

Past clients Over the years guests have included Somerset Maugham, Elizabeth Taylor, Noël Coward, Michael Jackson and Rudyard Kipling. The Raffles Museum is on the second floor,

with Raffles Hotel memorabilia, a must-see for anyone nostalgic about the golden age of travel. The nearby Jubilee Hall presents a multimedia show on the hotel's history four times a day. Some 70 specialist shops adjoin the main building.

Night Safari

Singapore's Night Safari—a zoo that allows you to see nocturnal animals— is the largest attraction of its kind in the world. Special lights that simulate moonlight were developed to illuminate this night zoo.

A world of animals The night safari is divided into eight "geographical" zones that are home to the park's 142 species—more than 1,000 animals in all. You can expect to see animals from the Southeast Asian rainforests, the African savanna, the Nepalese river valley, the South American pampas and the jungles of Myanmar (Burma). As in the Singapore Zoo, the enclosures are "open" and animals are confined by hidden walls and ditches. Five of these zones have walking tracks; others must be visited by tram.

Welcome to the jungle The best way to see the Night Safari is to take the tram journey—the tram is silent to avoid frightening the animals. A guide offers commentary as you pass through. Get off at the tram stations and follow the marked walking trails through each zone. You can rejoin the tram anytime; all follow the same route. Avoid using a flash on our camera as it disturbs the animals and fellow visitors.

The favorites Listen for the intermittent roaring of the big cats. The Leopard Trail is one of the busiest walking trails. You can see straight into the enclosure of the prowling leopards—only a plate-glass wall separates you from them. On the Mangrove Walk, fruit bats hang overhead in the gloom, and the elephants, giraffes, tigers and lions are always favorites. Be sure to catch the educational and entertaining "Creatures of the Night" show.

HIGHLIGHTS

- "Open" enclosures
- Leopard Trail
- Silent tram ride with commentary
- Mouse deer
- Tapirs
- Giraffes
- Lions
- Tigers
- Hippos
- Elephants
- Bats
- Walking trails

INFORMATION

www.zoo.com.sg/safari
- Off map to northwest
- Mandai Lake Road
- 6269 3411
- Daily 7.30pm–midnight
- Restaurant
- Ang Mo Kio MRT, then bus 138 or Choa Chu Kang MRT, then bus 927
- Reasonable
- Expensive
- Singapore Zoo (➤ 33), Mandai Orchid Gardens (➤ 45)

27

Chinatown

One of the best times to visit Chinatown is just before Chinese New Year, when the crowded streets throb with drumbeats and colorful stands sell everything from waxed ducks to *hong bao*, red packets for giving money as presents.

Singapore's Chinatown This area covers the streets leading off South Bridge Road between Maxwell Road and the Singapore River. As a policy, conservation of the old buildings goes hand-in-hand with new development here, and though an improvement over destruction, the often rather cosmetic results and years of unsympathetic infilling have left only a few streets with the authentic atmosphere and activities of old Chinatown.

What to see Erskine Road and Ann Siang Hill exhibit some of the best efforts of preservation. Temple, Pagoda and Trengganu streets have many traditional shophouses and coffee shops. People's Park Complex, on Eu Tong Sen Street, offers a wide range of goods, some very local in character, such as Chinese herbs and good jewelry. East of South Bridge Road, along Lorong Telok and Circular Road, are some examples of nicely decaying shophouses that have yet to feel the hand of the conservationist. Telok Ayer Street, although much renovated, is also worth a visit. Thian Hock Keng Temple (the Temple of Heavenly Happiness) is the oldest and most beautiful Chinese temple in the city. After years of restoration, it now welcomes visitors again. The original temple was built in 1840 by Hokkien immigrants grateful for a safe journey. Far East Square includes Fuk Tak Ch'i, a former temple that now houses a museum dedicated to Singapore's Chinese immigrants.

Lanterns hanging outside Chinese temple

Little India

Along Serangoon Road and the surrounding streets you can snatch all the sensations of India. Exotic aromas fill the air. Baskets overflow with spices. Stores are packed with colorful cloth. Many of these streets have not changed for decades.

Origins of Little India In the mid-19th century, lime pits and brick kilns were set up in the area, and it is thought that these attracted Singapore's Indians, who were laborers for the most part, to Serangoon Road. The swampy grasslands here were also good for raising cattle, another traditional occupation of the Indian community.

Little India today The district remains overwhelmingly Indian, full of sari-clad and Punjabi-suited women, spice shops, jasmine-garland sellers, Hindu temples and restaurants. Architectural gems abound. Apart from the crowded, lively streets and the tempting food emporiums, there is also the huge Zhujiao food market at the beginning of Serangoon Road; upstairs clothes and luggage are for sale. Across from the market, a little way up Serangoon Road, Komala Vilas restaurant (▶65) serves wonderful *dosai* (savory pancakes) and *thali* (mixed curries)—all vegetarian—as well as delicious Indian sweets such as milk *barfi*. Walk along Serangoon Road and you will come to Sri Veeramakaliamman Temple, dedicated to the ferocious goddess Kali. Farther on still is the Sri Srinivasa Perumal Temple with its magnificent 1979 *gopuram* (ornamental gateway). Take a detour to Race Course Road for a selection of Indian banana-leaf restaurants (▶65), notably those offering fish-head curry and a great selection of vegetable curries.

HIGHLIGHTS

- Sari shops
- Banana-leaf meals
- Fish-head curry
- Perfumed garlands
- Fortune-tellers
- Temples
- Spice shops
- Gold merchants

Ornate detail in Little India

INFORMATION

- ✚ E5
- ✉ Serangoon Road
- 🍴 Many restaurants and cafés
- Ⓜ Bugis
- 🚌 8, 13, 20, 23, 26, 31, 64, 65, 66, 67, 81, 90, 97, 103, 106, 111, 125, 131, 133, 139, 142, 147, 151, 154, 865
- Free
- Kampung Glam (▶47)   29

Asian Civilisations Museum

HIGHLIGHTS

- Chinese history timeline
- *Nonya* porcelain
- Red bat motifs
- Buddhist statues
- Literati gallery
- Jade collection
- Qing Dynasty porcelain
- Kang tables
- Islamic collection

INFORMATION

www.nhb.gov.sg/acm
- E6; E7
- 39 Armenian Street; 1 Empress Place
- 6332 3015; 6332 7789
- Mon 1–7, Tue–Sun 9–7, (Fri until 9)
- Empress Place: café, restaurant
- City Hall; Raffles Place
- 14, 16, 36, 65, 77, 124, 133, 167, 171, 190
- Good
- Inexpensive (free admission Fri 6–9)
- Fort Canning Park (➤ 36)
- Free guided tours Mon 2pm, Tue–Fri 11am, 2pm; Sat–Sun 11am, 2pm, 3.30pm. Museum shops. Temporary exhibitions

Displaying relics of mainland China, continental India, Islamic West Asia and Southeast Asian cultures this excellent museum is housed in two of Singapore's finest and most presitgious colonial buildings.

Past and present development In 1997, the beautiful Tao Nan School, which dates from 1910, was restored to house the first phase of the Asian Civilisations Museum. The second phase of development, completed in 2003, involved the renovation of the imposing 1865 Empress Place building as the museum's second wing. The museums present a fascinating, inspiring insight into Asia, its historical development and rich artistic traditions. This is one of three museums run by the National Heritage Board; the other two are the Singapore History Museum (reopening in 2006), a three-minute walk away, and the prestigious Singapore Art Museum (➤ 46).

New extension The Empress Place building, with 11 galleries over three levels houses over 1,300 artifacts from the museum's collections on the civilizations of China, Southeast Asia and West Asian (Islamic). The story of Asia is showcased with static displays, interactive exhibits and multimedia.

Stunning displays At Armenian Street you can view what is arguably the world's best display on Peranakan culture. The Peranakans were known as the "King's Chinese," holding key posts in the administration. The fine collection of silver, porcelain and jewelry is complemented by ornate furniture, with its central display the re-creation of a monumental altar from a wealthy Peranakan family.

Botanic Gardens

Don't leave Singapore without a visit to this 128-acre (52-ha) botanical treasure-trove with its wonderful National Orchid Garden. It is best explored in the relative cool of the morning or the evening.

Botanical beginnings Singapore's tranquil botanic gardens are only a few minutes from frenetic Orchard Road. Here some half a million species grow in a variety of landscapes from rolling lawns to orchid gardens and tropical rainforest. Raffles established botanical gardens at the base of Government Hill (Fort Canning) in 1822, and the collection was moved to its present site in 1859, at a time when tigers still roamed the area. Over the decades the gardens have been enlarged and landscaped. In 1877 one of the gardens' early directors, "Mad" Henry Ridley (who earned his nickname for his evangelistic promotion of the rubber industry) propagated the first rubber trees in Asia, from which the earliest plantations on the Malay Peninsula were established. He is also known for developing a way to tap latex that did not kill the tree. Descendants of those first trees, native to Brazil, are still found in the gardens. In the 1960s the gardens supplied many of the seedlings for roadsides and parks all over the island, and the greening of Singapore began.

Attractions There is an extensive collection of orchids and many members of the diverse and useful palm family, including coconut, sago and lontar. The gardens are popular with locals, who jog, picnic and attend the frequent open-air concerts in Palm Valley. Attractions include the National Orchid Garden, the visitor center, a cool house for high-altitude orchids, spice gardens and an eco-lake.

HIGHLIGHTS

- Rubber trees
- Bandstand
- *Cyrtostachys renda* (sealing-wax palm)
- National Orchid Garden
- Jungle Walk
- Palm Valley
- *Myristica fragans* (nutmeg tree)
- *Cinnamomum zeylanicum* (cinnamon tree)
- Topiary
- Bamboos
- Herbarium

INFORMATION

www.nparks.gov.sg

- ✚ A5
- ✉ Junction of Cluny and Holland roads
- ☎ 6471 7361
- 🕐 Daily 5am–midnight; National Orchid Garden daily 8.30am–7pm
- 🍴 Visitor center restaurant and café; vending machine; hawker center outside main gates
- Ⓜ MRT to Orchard, then SBS bus 7, 106, 123 or 174
- 🚌 As above, plus 75, 105
- ♿ Good
- 💲 Botanic Gardens free, admission to Orchid Garden inexpensive
- ↔ Orchard Road (▶ 32, 72–73)
- ❓ Outdoor concerts; leaflets available from the visitor center

31

Orchard Road

HIGHLIGHTS

- Specialist shops
- Exclusive designer shops
- Coffee shops
- Borders bookshop
- Books Kinokuniya
- Takashimaya
- Sushi in the basement

INFORMATION

- ✚ C5; D6; E6
- ✉ Ngee Ann City, Orchard Road
- ⏰ Daily 10–9.30. Restaurants on upper floors 10am–11pm
- 🍴 Restaurants, food courts, supermarket
- 🚇 Orchard
- 🚌 7, 14, 16, 65, 106, 111, 123, 167, 605
- ♿ Good
- 💲 Free
- ❓ Post office, with overseas delivery; customer service center; SISTIC outlet; banks

One of the world's great shopping boulevards, Orchard Road is the retail heart and soul of Singapore. Day or night, a stroll from one end to the other is a pleasure, even if you don't spend a penny; it is a people-watchers' delight.

Room to move Wide sidewalks and plenty of potential coffee stops help make encountering the cosmopolitan charms of Orchard Road a pleasure. And escaping the extreme heat that this equatorial city experiences is as easy as dashing into one of the dozens of air-conditioned shopping malls that line the street. Goods from all parts of the world are on offer, including well-priced electrical items, designer fashions, antiques and gifts. Inexpensive food courts are prevalent and there are any number of good restaurants. For a fine walking tour, start at Centrepoint, near Somerset Station and walk to Tanglin Mall at the western end of the street. On the way, pause near the intersection with Scotts Road to drop in at Borders bookstore, or take in a film at the nearby Lido. Stores are open until 10pm.

Ngee Ann City The most impressive of Singapore's many shopping malls, this complex is especially popular because of its wide range of supplementary services: banks, restaurants, food courts, post office and supermarket. The stylish, pricey anchor store, Takashimaya, offers departmental shopping at its best, with lovely goods and Singapore's best food hall, where sushi is a top seller. Books Kinokuniya, Southeast Asia's largest bookstore and the plethora of the top-of-the-line brand-name shops such as Chanel, Cartier and Tiffany, are additional draws. The plaza in front of the building buzzes on weekends.

Singapore Zoo

Treetops Trail, a wooden walkway 20ft (6m) off the ground, lets you join the gibbons and a troop of cheeky red langurs for a monkey's-eye view of a simulated rainforest. Watch the endearing langurs as they feed, groom and play.

Abandoned pets Singapore's zoo, acclaimed as one of the finest in the world, is also one of the youngest. Its beginnings can be traced back to the 1960s, when British forces pulled out of Singapore and left a ragbag of family pets behind. The zoo, which sprawls over 69 acres (28ha), was officially opened in 1973 and is now home to more than 412 species, some endangered and rare, such as tigers, orang-utans, Komodo dragons and golden lion tamarins. Breeding programs have been initiated for endangered species, with some success.

Polar bears and pygmy hippos Living conditions are as near as possible to those in the wild— mini-habitats bounded by naturalistic trenches, moats and rock walls. More than 2,900 animals can be seen, none more popular than the orang-utans with whom you can have breakfast or tea, consisting of a human-style meal, apparently enjoyed by the apes. Polar bears, otters and pygmy hippos can be seen close up from underwater viewing areas, and the islands constructed for the different primates provide a clear view of these generally hydrophobic creatures. The snake house is very popular with children and the tiger enclosure is always crowded. There is a great deal to see, and if you get tired, you can always jump onto the silent tram that loops around the fine landscaped grounds, or take in one of the shows designed to entertain those not content with seeing sea lions, elephants and chimpanzees doing what comes naturally.

HIGHLIGHTS

- "Open" enclosures
- Tigers
- Pygmy hippos
- Primate islands
- Air-conditioned shelters
- Treetops Trail
- Komodo dragons
- Children's World
- Animal shows
- Tram

INFORMATION

- www.zoo.com.sg
- Off map to northwest
- 80 Mandai Lake Road
- 6269 3411
- Daily 8.30–6
- Restaurants
- MRT to Ang Mo Kio then SBS bus 138, or MRT to Choa Chu Kang then TIBS 927
- SBS bus 171 to Mandai Road then cross road and take 138 or 927
- Good
- Moderate
- Mandai Orchid Gardens (➤ 45)
- Jungle breakfast with orang-utans 9–10am, afternoon tea 4–4.30pm (reservations necessary); animal shows 2.30–3.30pm

Sentosa Island

INFORMATION

- ✛ Off map to south
- ✉ Sentosa Island
- ☎ Sentosa Information Centre 6275 0388; www. sentosa.com. Sentosa Golf Club 6275 0022
- ◷ Mon–Thu 7am–11pm, Fri–Sun, public hols 7.30am–midnight
- ¶¶ Cafés and restaurants
- ☒ Cable car from World Trade Centre (WTC) and Mount Faber
- ☐ To reach WTC (Telok Blangah Road): 10, 30, 61, 65, 84, 93, 97, 100, 131, 143, 145, 166, 176, 855. To reach Sentosa direct: bus A from WTC bus terminal, bus C from Tiong Bahru MRT station, bus E from Orchard Road. Last bus from Sentosa: Mon–Thu 10.30pm; Fri, Sun, public hols 12.30am
- 🖃 From WTC ferry terminal
- ♿ Few
- 💲 Expensive. Free transport on Sentosa
- ↔ Mount Faber Park (► 58–59)

Even in clean and tidy Singapore the perfect order of Sentosa Island is incredible. You will either love or hate the wholesome family package of attractions, but give it a day and you may well enjoy making up your mind.

Getting there A former pirate lair and British military base, this island playground now attracts more than four million visitors a year. Sentosa can be reached across a causeway or by a cable car that runs just over one mile (1.5km) from the 380-ft (116-m) high Mt. Faber. The station is at the World Trade Centre.

For the active Rent a canoe or windsurfer, play a round on Serapong Golf Course (weekdays only), follow the well-signed walks and bicycle routes or relax on its 2 miles (3km) of beaches.

Adventure Watch a volcano erupt every half-hour in VolcanoLand and visit Lost Civilizations, Asian Village or Fantasy Island, which offers 13 water rides and 32 water slides. See more than 350 tropical marine species at Underwater World (feeding times are 11.30, 2.30, 4.30), insects galore at Insect Kingdom and more than 2,500 types of lepidoptera in Butterfly Park. Audiovisuals and waxworks relate the nation's history in Images of Singapore. Sentosa's Maritime Museum is agreeably low-tech. Visit in the evening for the laser and fountain shows, and check out the spotlighted Enchanted Grove gnome garden.

Jurong BirdPark

Hundreds of penguins and puffins crowded together on an icy beach is an unexpected sight just a few miles from the equator. And don't miss the Waterfall Aviary, where tropical bird species fly almost free.

The world's birds Jurong BirdPark is Asia-Pacific's biggest bird park—49 acres (20ha)—and home to more than 8,000 birds, many from the tropics. Some 600 species, from all over the world, are housed in aviaries and other apparently open enclosures.

Birds of a feather Not far from the entrance, penguins live in a simulated Antarctic habitat with a swimming area. The vast glass-sided tank has windows 98ft (30m) wide. The Waterfall Aviary is the most spectacular area, with 5 acres (2 ha) of forest

contained beneath high netting, with more than 1,500 tropical birds. The aviary also has a 98-ft (30-m) man-made waterfall. A monorail gives a good overview of the park, but it's well worth getting off, to see the birds close up. The Southeast Asian Birds Aviary re-creates a rainforest, complete with midday storm, and contains more than 260 species, including the colorful parrots. Jungle Jewels is a large walk-through aviary devoted to hummingbirds and other South American species. There birds of prey and parrots shows are also entertaining. When you have finished watching birds, cross the road and take a look at the reptile park.

HIGHLIGHTS

- Penguin feeding time
- Jungle Jewels
- Pelican Lake
- Monorail trip
- Waterfall Aviary
- World of Darkness
- Crowned pigeons
- Birds of paradise
- Southeast Asian hornbills and South American toucans
- Southeast Asian Birds Aviary

INFORMATION

www.birdpark.com.sg
- ✚ Off map to west
- ✉ 2 Jurong Hill
- ☎ 6265 0022
- ◉ Daily 9–5
- 🍴 McDonald's, Waterfall Kiosk, PFS Terrace Kiosk
- 🚇 MRT to Boon Lay then SBS bus 194 or 251
- ♿ Good
- 💲 Moderate
- ⟷ Singapore Science Centre (► 44), Chinese and Japanese Gardens (► 58)
- ❓ Bird shows: All-Star Show (11am, 3pm), Birds of Prey (10am, 4pm), Penguin Parade (10.30am, 3.30pm)

White-throated kingfisher

Fort Canning Park

HIGHLIGHTS

- Christian cemetery
- Keramat Iskandar Shah
- Fort's Gothic gateway
- Spice garden
- *Bougainvillaea campa*
- Battle Box (World War II bunker)

INFORMATION

www.nparks.gov.sg

- E6
- Off Canning Rise
- 6332 1200
- Daily 24 hours
- Restaurant at Fort Canning Country Club
- Dhoby Ghaut
- 7, 14, 16, 32, 36, 37, 97, 103, 124, 131, 166, 167, 171, 174, 190
- None
- Free
- Clarke Quay and Riverside Point (➤ 40)

Fort Canning's gateway

This area, known during the 19th century as Government Hill, is a historic high point—quite literally. From the gold finds of the 14th-century to Stamford Raffles' house and a late-19th-century fort, this hill has seen many changes in the past 600 years.

Historic hill When Raffles landed in Singapore this hill was known by its Malay name of Bukit Larangan, meaning Forbidden Hill, for it was here that the Malay kings were buried. A Muslim shrine, Keramat Iskandar Shah, was also found on the site, as was Javanese gold of the 14th century, a sign of Java's wide-reaching influence at that time. With a commanding view of the harbor and settlement, it was a prime location and was quickly chosen to be the site for Government House (the governor's residence). Its slopes were given over to Raffles' experimental garden with its variety of economically useful plants, particularly spices.

Transformations The house was demolished in the mid-19th century and a fort built, named for Viscount Canning, a governor of India. The fort, too, was demolished, in 1907, to make way for a reservoir; all that remains is the Gothic gateway. On the eastern side of the hill are remnants of an old Christian cemetery. The government offices at the top, built in 1926, now house the Fort Canning Centre and accommodate a professional dance troupe, exhibition space and a theater. You can also visit the bunker where the British Malaya Command had its headquarters in World War II.

The Padang

The word *padang* is Malay for "plain," and that is just what this is. Although unrelieved by trees or hills, these few acres offer a good breathing space and act as a focal point for the colonial buildings grouped around it.

Recreation Once the Padang directly faced the sea, but land reclamation in Marina Bay has long since changed its outlook. The Padang, which goes back to Raffles' days, has retained its use as a recreational area. Cricket and rugby matches are played—in season, of course—and while non-members may not venture into the clubs at either end of the Padang, they can stand and watch the games. St. Andrew's Cathedral, behind the Padang, was completed in 1861 with Indian convict labor. City Hall, facing the Padang, has seen several historic events: the herding of Europeans onto the Padang on the morning of the Japanese occupation, and the formal surrender of the Japanese on its steps in 1945.

Nearby buildings At the southern end is the Cricket Club, with a commanding view of the Padang. The group of government buildings includes the attorney-general's chambers (resembling a small opera house), the Victoria Theatre and Concert Hall buildings, and the former Parliament House. Turning back down Connaught Drive and Esplanade Park, you will see the outline of Suntec City—a massive conference and exhibition center—and a group of hotels built on reclaimed land, together with Marina Square Shopping Centre. At the northern end of the Padang is the Recreation Club, originally built in 1885 for Eurasians, who were excluded from the Cricket Club.

HIGHLIGHTS

- City Hall steps
- Singapore Cricket Club
- Cricket and rugby matches
- Victoria Theatre portico
- Old Parliament House
- Esplanade Walk
- St. Andrew's Cathedral
- Statue of Raffles

INFORMATION

- ✚ F7
- ✉ St. Andrew's Road
- 🚇 City Hall
- 🚌 10, 70, 75, 82, 97, 100, 107, 125, 130, 131, 167, 196
- ♿ None
- 🎟 Free
- ↔ Raffles Hotel (▶ 26), Fort Canning Park (▶ 36), Boat Quay (▶ 38)

Westin Stamford Hotel

Boat Quay

The bundles of rattan and sacks of rice have long disappeared, as have the boatmen, but the sweep of shophouses, the thronging crowds and the odd tour operator's bumboat give an inkling of an earlier life along the Singapore River.

Early Days After decades as a sleepy backwater, Boat Quay has sprung back to life. For a century after the founding of Singapore, Bu Ye Tian, as the Chinese used to call it, was "a place of ceaseless activity" with little wooden bumboats and sampans ferrying their cargoes of rubber and rice, cotton and rattan, sago and spices, back and forth to ships at Tanjong Pagar Docks. The riverbank was lined with shophouses, which served as combined trading offices, homes and godowns, the warehouses used for storage and sorting. Behind this area was Commercial Square, now Raffles Place, where the big international shipping and trading companies had their commercial offices.

Changes With the opening of Singapore's large container port facilities, the bumboats departed Boat Quay and the area was left to a few traders and mechanics who continued to eke out a living there. Then, in the late 1980s, Boat Quay was designated a conservation area and life was dramatically restored to the river bank. A riverside walkway was built and the shophouses were renovated.

Active once more Bars, nightclubs and restaurants now fill the area and the riverside is awash with tables and chairs for outdoor dining. Boat Quay today is lively and picturesque—a pleasant place for a meal with views across to Empress Place, and on to the impressive skyscrapers of the financial district.

Esplanade—Theatres on the Bay

Singapore's stunning new waterfront theater and entertainment complex, dubbed the Durians for its two striking domes, represents the government's serious attempt to attract world-class performers and the best local talent.

Cutting-edge architecture The S$600-million Esplanade is seen by Singaporeans as part of their coming of age from economic prosperity to regional arts excellence. The architect's challenge, given the tropical climate and the desire to present patrons with a dramatic view of the surroundings, was to design an essentially glazed building that was protected from the sun and heat. The resultant fixed exterior triangular aluminum sun shields, set to be opened or closed, depending on the angle of the sun, were the final design solution.

World-class facilities Opened in 2002, the Esplanade includes The Concert Hall with 1,600 seats and a 200-seat choir stall; the Lyric Theatre seating 2,000, modelled on a traditional Italian opera house with one stall and three tiers; and a smaller theater for drama, dance and recital with 750 seats. Internal venues were designed to accommodate the louder and more percussive styles of Asian performances, although the flexible acoustics also suits Western orchestras. The two main outdoor performance spaces and several lesser ones reflect the Asian preference for outdoor entertainment.

Shopping and dining Esplanade Mall, on three levels, offers a diverse retail mix from fashion to flowers, home decorations to handmade pottery, and there are several premier restaurants and specialty cafes and bars with views overlooking the waterfront and CBD surrounds.

HIGHLIGHTS

- Twin glass domes
- Waterfront vistas
- High-quality performances
- Stunning concert hall
- Free performances
- Excellent restaurants
- Esplanade Mall shopping

INFORMATION

- ✛ F7
- ✉ 1 Esplanade Drive
- ☎ 6828 2222
- ◷ Daily 10–10
- 🍴 Cafés, restaurants
- 🚇 City Hall
- ♿ Good
- 🎫 Free entry; tours moderate
- ↔ Raffles Hotel (▶ 26), The Padang (▶ 37)
- ❓ Guided tours (45 mins) in English Mon–Fri 11am, 2pm, Sat, Sun 11am

Aerial View

Clarke Quay & Riverside Point

HIGHLIGHTS

- Riverfront walk
- Street stalls
- Bandstand
- River trip
- Brewerkz
- Flea market

INFORMATION

www.clarkequay.com.sg

- ✚ bI; E7
- ✉ 3 River Valley Road
- ☎ 6227 8001
- 🍴 Numerous
- Ⓜ Raffles Place
- 🚌 SBS bus 54 from Scotts Road; 32, 195 from City Hall MRT
- ♿ Few
- ▨ Free
- ↔ Fort Canning Park (► 36), Sri Mariamman Temple (► 42)
- ❓ *Wayang* (Chinese opera) at Gas Lamp Square on Wed and Fri evenings from 7.30–8.30

These prime riverside destinations, five blocks of godowns and shophouses featuring restaurants and pubs, specialty shops and car-free streets, come alive in the evenings and on the weekend.

Regeneration Once a riverside area of old wharves and warehouses destined for refurbishment, Clarke Quay, along Singapore River, has been transformed by one of Singapore's most ambitious restoration schemes. The quay is named after Sir Andrew Clarke, governor of the Straits Settlements from 1873 to 1875. The area was covered with godowns constructed between 1860 and 1920 by European and Chinese entrepreneurs. The new Clarke Quay opened in 1993 with brand-new godowns, shophouses and trading posts constructed along the riverfront and in the streets leading up to River Valley Road. A colorful junk that doubles as a restaurant is moored in the river.

Shopping and eating The entire area is given over to shops and eateries—you can buy everything from pottery and leather goods to wooden clogs, batik prints and Chinese medicines. Outdoor dining is popular, just as at Boat Quay farther downriver (► 38. A carnival atmosphere prevails year-round, with street stalls and a bandstand complete with entertainment. The Sunday flea market has become a popular among toy collectors, although prices can be high. If you cross the Read or Ord bridges to the opposite bank, you'll find Riverside Point, with shops, a cinema, good restaurants and the Brewerkz microbrewery. Here you will also find exhibitions about the Singapore River hosted by the Singapore History Museum while their Stamford Road premises are being renovated.

Bukit Timah Nature Reserve

The exhilarating walk up Singapore's highest hill offers a glimpse of the majestic rainforest that once dominated the island. Bukit Timah is one of the few areas left in Singapore where the natural landscape remains pristine.

Singapore rainforest The last remaining area of primary tropical rainforest in Singapore covers 410 acres (166ha) of Bukit Timah (Malay for "tin hill"), which at 535 ft (163m) is the island's highest point. The forest has never been logged and, apart from three quarries on its borders, is virgin forest, little changed over the millennia.

Flora Trails that start at the visitor center allow you to observe the reserve's fauna and flora. Among the highlights are the splendid dipterocarps—a family of trees almost all of which were originally found only in Malaysia—some nearly 100ft (30m) tall. Lianas and rattans trail and twist though the forest, and strangler figs can be found. The latter are so called because they begin life high in the crown of trees and grow aerial roots down to the ground, gradually encircling the host tree; deprived of sunlight at its top and soil nutrients at its base, the tree eventually dies. Smaller epiphytes, with such apt names as bird's-nest fern and staghorn fern, emerge from trunks and branches looking like unkempt bushes.

Fauna Animals are more difficult to spot, except for the marauding macaques, which gather at the base of the reserve and menace for a fight if you get too close—so don't! Visit in early morning for the greatest chance of spotting wildlife. Animals you are most likely to see include squirrels, lizards and birds such as the greater racket-tailed drongo and the banded woodpecker.

HIGHLIGHTS

- Visitor center
- Winding forest trails
- Rainforest trees
- Strangler figs
- Pitcher plants
- Ferns
- Fungi
- Macaques
- Tree shrews
- Giant ants

INFORMATION

www.nparks.gov.sg
- Off map to northwest
- 177 Hindhede Drive
- 1800 471 7300
- Daily 8–6
- MRT to Newton then SBS bus 171 or TIBS 182
- 65, 67, 75, 170, 171, 852, 961
- None
- Free
- Visitor center display and bookshop open daily 8.30–6

Sri Mariamman Temple

HIGHLIGHTS

- *Gopuram*
- Thimithi festival
- Main doors
- Principal hall
- Ceiling frescoes
- Shrines

INFORMATION

- ✚ bII; E8
- ✉ 244 South Bridge Road
- ☎ 6223 4064
- 🕐 Daily 7am–9pm
- 🚇 Tanjong Pagar
- 🚌 SBS bus 61, 103, 166, 197 from City Hall MRT
- ♿ None
- 💷 Free
- ↔ Chinatown (➤ 28)

A devotee burns incense in Sri Mariamman temple

This is Singapore's oldest Hindu temple, a technicolor shrine with brilliant statuary on the tower over the entrance. It is rather surprising to find it in the middle of Chinatown, but there has long been a Hindu temple here.

Origins The first temple was erected in 1827 by Nariana Pillai, Singapore's first Indian immigrant who became a successful trader and leader of the Hindu community. The original temple, made of wood and *atap* (nipa-palm leaves), was replaced by a brick structure in 1843. This building was later restored and extended. The temple is dedicated to the goddess Mariamman, who has powers to cure epidemics such as cholera and smallpox.

What to see This temple shows the three principal elements of Dravidian architecture: an interior shrine (*vimanam*) covered by a decorated dome, an assembly hall (*madapam*) used for prayers and an entrance tower (*gopuram*) covered with brightly painted Hindu deities. The splendid *gopuram* was not erected until 1903. The preferred venue of most Hindu weddings, the temple is also the focus for the annual Thimithi festival (➤ 4), when devotees walk across a pit of glowing coals—supposedly painless—to honor the Hindu goddess Draupathi. The temple is still very much a place of worship and you must respect this and remember to remove your footwear before entering.

Bugis Street

Bugis Village, a very pale imitation of the original Bugis Street, offers a sanitized version of the street life found in other Asian cities. Clubs and market stalls abound, and touts trap tourists into dining at expensive restaurants.

Yesterday Bugis Street was the sin hotspot of old Singapore, the haunt of prostitutes and transvestites. Such activities were disapproved of by the Singaporean authorities, and the street was demolished in the 1980s to make way for the Bugis MRT station. Remembered with affection and sought out in vain by visitors, it was rebuilt in 1991, 449ft (137m) from its original site. Six blocks of Chinese shophouses and some of the more celebrated original buildings were re-created and filled with pavement cafés and specialty shops.

Today The night market is open until late. Luxury goods, generally fake, tend to be sold near Victoria Street, and you can buy crafts and curios farther down the road, fruit and vegetables near Albert Street. Around the edge of Bugis Village are several fast-food outlets, shops selling the latest fashions, a tea specialist and a traditional herbalist.

Bugis Junction Above Bugis MRT station is the 15-floor Bugis Junction complex, consisting of retail outlets, a cinema and office complex. The old Hylam street shophouse facades have been re-created in bright colors, and the whole street has been covered with a glass roof. Air-conditioning provides temperatures that remind you of temperate places, so you can shop or sit in one of the many cafés in comfort. The Hotel Inter-Continental adjoins the Bugis Junction complex.

HIGHLIGHTS

- Boutiques
- Bugis Junction
- Chinese herbalist
- Hylam Street
- Night market
- Open-air restaurants

INFORMATION

- ✚ F6
- ✉ Bugis Street
- 🕐 Market open daily to midnight. Bars open daily to 2 or 3am
- ✉ Albert Street
- 🕐 Mon–Fri 8.30pm–2am, Sat, Sun 8.30pm–3am
- 🍴 Open-air restaurants, fast-food outlets
- 🚇 Bugis
- 🚌 2, 5, 7, 12, 32, 61, 62, 63, 84, 130, 160, 197, 520, 851, 960
- ♿ Few (pedestrian precinct)
- 💷 Moderate bars and food, antiques and crafts
- 🔁 Little India (► 29), Kampung Glam (► 47)

Singapore Science Centre

Hundreds of hands-on exhibits excite children and enlighten adults. The world of science and wonder awaits at the Singapore Science Centre, which houses more than 850 exhibits.

HIGHLIGHTS

- Atrium laser show
- Aviation Gallery
- Discovery Centre
- Hall of Information Technology
- Ecogarden
- Life Sciences Gallery
- Physical Sciences Gallery
- Omni Theatre

INFORMATION

www.science.edu.sg
- Off map to west
- 15 Science Centre Road
- 6425 2500
- SSC Tue–Sun, public hols 10–6. Omni Theatre Tue–Sun, public hols 10–8
- Café in SSC, fast food in Omni Theatre
- Jurong East then 500 yards (500m) walk (turn left from station, along Block 135) or bus 335
- 66, 178, 198 direct; 51, 78, 197 to Jurong East Interchange then 335 or walk
- Good (space for 10 wheelchairs in Omni Theatre)
- Inexpensive
- Jurong BirdPark (▶ 35), Chinese and Japanese Gardens (▶ 58)

Interactive exhibits The Singapore Science Centre opened its doors in 1977 and now attracts more than a million visitors each year. Exhibits in themed galleries offer fascinating insights into human achievements in the physical and life sciences. Many of the exhibits are interactive, and some are supported by talks and films.

Science to hand A laser light display welcomes you in the main lobby. The Aviation Gallery, introduces the principles of flight and examines how man first explored the skies. The Life Sciences Gallery focuses on the environment and people. You can walk through the internal organs of a human body in the Human Anatomy section. The Discovery Centre aims to stimulate the imagination of younger children with interactive displays, and the Ecogarden is informative for horticulturalists with its mini-orchard, hydroponic farm and medicinal garden. The Hall of Information Technology (1998) explains the role of communications in today's world.

Omni Theatre and Planetarium Next to the Science Centre is the Omni Theatre. This theater has a five-floor high, 75-ft (23-m) curved Omnimax screen, and state-of-the-art projection and audio equipment with surround sound. You can see films on subjects as diverse as climbing Mt. Everest and the rule of China's first emperors. The features change every six months, so check to find out what's on during your visit.

Mandai Orchid Gardens

Many of the orchid hybrids on display at these gardens are stunning, especially the _Vanda_ "Mandai Glow," with its beautiful blend of peach and pale orange.

Cultivation Orchids have been grown on this site since 1951, when the land was leased by a couple of enthusiasts, John Laycock and Lee Kim Hong. It wasn't until 1956 that the gardens were turned into a commercial venture. Following Laycock's death, Amy Ede, his adopted daughter, managed the gardens. The area under cultivation has increased over the years to 10 acres (4ha) and today the orchid gardens are the largest on the island. Millions of sprays are exported all over the world each year, kept in good condition using a unique technology developed by the owners.

The orchids The gardens are packed with gorgeous blooms, some native, some introduced, as well as the many hybrids that have been the making of the Singapore orchid industry. Amazingly, despite the vast array of species on display, all orchids have the same shape—three sepals and three petals, but one of the petals, known as the "lip," is a completely different shape from the others.

National flower The deep pink and white flowers of _Vanda_ "Miss Joaquim," Singapore's national flower, can be seen in abundance, as can many other varieties, including delicate slipper orchids and fantastic moth orchids. An hour's stroll in the gardens, which also contain a landscaped water garden, makes a gentle start to the day.

HIGHLIGHTS

- Early morning fragrance
- Black orchid
- Tiger orchid
- _Oncidium_ "Golden Shower"
- Torch ginger
- Jade vine

INFORMATION

- 🞢 Off map to northwest
- ✉ Mandai Lake Road
- ☎ 6269 1036
- 🕐 Daily 8.30–5.30
- 🚇 MRT to Ang Mo Kio then SBS bus 138
- 🚌 SBS bus 171 to Mandai Road, then cross road for 138, or TIBS 927
- ♿ None
- 💲 Inexpensive
- ↔ Singapore Zoo (► 33), Night Safari (► 27)
- ❓ Boxed orchids can be sent abroad–details in shop

45

Singapore Art Museum

INFORMATION

www.nhb.gov.sg
- E6
- 71 Bras Basah Road
- 6332 3222
- Daily 10–7 (Fri 10–9)
- Dome café adjacent
- City Hall
- 14, 16, 36, 56, 82, 100, 107, 125, 167
- Few
- Inexpensive, free admission Fri 6–9
- Fort Canning Park (► 36)
- Free guided tours Tue–Fri 11am, 2pm, Sat, Sun 11am, 2pm, 3.30pm. Museum shop

With its focus on art of the 20th century, this is Singapore's flagship art museum dedicated to the collection and display of contemporary works from Singapore and Southeast Asia. It also presents traveling exhibitions.

National treasure The museum, opened in 1996, is housed in the restored 19th-century St. Joseph's Insititution building, a former Catholic boys' school, and displays Singapore's national art collection. The permanent collection has grown from under 2,000 artworks to over 6,000, and now houses the largest and most comprehensive collection of 20th-century Southeast Asian art in the region.

State of the art Almost 107,600sq ft (10,000sq m) of floor space include 14 galleries, a reference library, an auditorium, a multipurpose hall, a museum shop, courtyards and an electronic E-image Gallery that runs interactive programs featuring some of the museum's collection on a large visual monitor. Check out the nearby café that looks out over Queens Street.

On show Along with "Imaging Selves," the Singapore Art Museum's first exhibition showcasing its permanent collection, the museum has also curated country focus exhibitions, "From There to Now" and "Soul Ties: The Land & Her People," focusing on Malaysia and Indonesia. An overview of Singaporean art is on permanent display and traveling exhibitions expose the region internationally. A community program covers a diversity of art trends and practices, fringe activities and lectures. Check out Georgette Chen's striking *Self Portrait* (1934) and Chong Fah Cheong's tongue-in-cheek *Family and One* (1985).

Kampung Glam

The impressive golden domes and minarets of Sultan Mosque, glinting in the late afternoon sun, and the call of the muezzin, remind you that this area of Singapore is very much part of the Islamic world.

In the past Kampung Glam, where the Sultan of Singapore lived, was set aside in the early days for Malays, Arab, and Bugis traders. The "Glam" may be named after the *gelam* tree from which medicinal oil was produced. Kampung Glam is now part of a conservation area.

Today Although there are 80 mosques on the island, Sultan Mosque is the focus of worship for Singapore's Muslim (mainly Malay) community. There has been a mosque on this site since 1824, when the East India Company made a grant for its construction. The present mosque dates from 1928, and reveals an interesting mix of Middle Eastern and Moorish influences. Its gilded dome is impressive; unusually, its base is made from bottles. Seen as you walk up Bussorah Street, with its shophouses at the rear, the mosque is truly stunning. Visitors are welcome outside prayer times, as long as they are well covered—no shorts. The *istana* (palace), built in the 1840s, is at the top of Sultan Gate and is well worth a look. The surrounding streets are good sources for *souk* items like basketware, perfume, batik and leather goods. The nearby Muslim coffee shops serve a wide range of Indian Muslim dishes such as *murtabak* (pancake with various fillings) and *mee goreng* (spicy fried noodles).

HIGHLIGHTS

- Bussorah Street
- Gilded dome of Sultan Mosque
- Prayer hall
- Istana Kampung Glam
- *Murtabak*
- Batik

INFORMATION

Sultan Mosque
- F6
- 3 Muscat Street
- 6293 4405
- Daily 11–7
- Numerous coffee shops
- Bugis
- 2, 32, 51, 61, 63, 84, 133, 145, 197
- None
- Free
- Raffles Hotel (➤ 26), Bugis Street (➤ 43)

Rainbow hues for sale

East Coast Park

HIGHLIGHTS

- Big Splash water rides
- Canoe rental
- East Coast Sailing Centre
- Parkland Golf Driving Range
- Tennis center
- White-sand beaches

INFORMATION

- ✚ H6–N6
- ✉ East Coast Service Road
- ☎ ECSC 6449 5118. Regent Bowl 6443 1518. Tennis Centre 6442 5966. Parkland Golf Range 6440 6726. Big Splash 6345 6762. Europa 6447 0869. Crocodilarium 6447 6439. Ponggol Seafood 6448 8511
- 🍽 East Coast Lagoon Food Centre hawker center (► 67), various kiosks, fast food at ECRC and Big Splash
- 🚌 Bedok then bus 401 or bus 31, 197; Eunos then 55, 155; Paya Lebar then 76, 135 and walk
- 🚍 16, 31, 55, 76, 135, 155, 196, 197, 853 daily to Marine Parade Road; 401 to East Coast Service Road (Sun)
- ♿ Some level paths
- 💲 Free; rental charges per hour for sports, etc.
- ↔ Changi Chapel (► 20), Joo Chiat Road (► 49)

Two decades of land reclamation have created this beachside playground. Swim or sail; walk, jog or cycle the 6 miles (10km) of tracks between coconut groves; or laze on white sands with views of Indonesia's Riau Islands.

Plenty to do Picnicking families flock to the area on the weekends. There are many places to rent a bicycle, canoe, rollerblades or a deck chair, and it's a pleasant place to relax and catch a cooling breeze in the evening. The seafood center at the Urban Development and Management Corporation (UDMC) clubhouse is popular with those who appreciate good seafood.

East Coast Sailing Centre Sailboards and laser dinghies can be rented here. If you encounter difficulties at sea, a rescue boat is on hand to bring you back to the East Coast Sailing Centre. The UDMC clubhouse has sports equipment for rent.

East Coast Recreation Centre Next to the park at the East Coast Recreation Centre are clay tennis courts (open until late evening), two bowling alleys and a snooker and billiards hall (open until the early hours). Golfers can practice at the two-tier, 163-yard (150-m) Parkland for just the cost of the balls. You can also rent bicycles, rollerblades and canoes. At the Big Splash, water rides delight adults and children alike, and in the same complex local bands entertain at the Europa each evening.

Singapore Crocodilarium Approximately 1,000 crocodiles, crammed into concrete tanks, can be found at the Crocodilarium, where they are farmed. Crocodile-skin products are also showcased in the shop here.

Joo Chiat Road

Wonderful original architecture and intriguing old businesses by day, and an exciting mix of restaurants and music lounges in the evening, give a fascinating glimpse of former times and a sample of Singapore life today.

History The development of Katong was begun after World War I by Chew Joo Chiat. This once quiet seaside village is today an eclectic mix of colonial villas, Peranakan-style terraces and Malay bungalows. Some are preserved, many are being renovated, others remain untouched. The Joo Chiat Complex, at the northern end of Joo Chiat near the Malay Village (➤ 77), is a busy local shopping complex selling fabrics and household goods at bargain prices. Next to the Village is the Geylang Serai market, a traditional Asian market, a good place to browse.

Ecletic mix Opposite Guan Hoe Soon Restaurant (which serves traditional Peranakan *nonya* dishes) is a typical 1920s corner terrace, with an ornate frieze of green dragons on the roof pediment. Terrace houses with covered walkways can be found along the road. The second stories may be pillared verandas (No. 113), or have ornate casement windows (Nos. 370–6). Colorful tiles are a common feature (Nos. 137–9). Koon Seng Road, to the left, has two facing rows of bright terrace houses with courtyard gardens in front and extravagant moldings, tiles and paintwork. Set in dense gardens are Malay-style elevated bungalows (Nos. 229, 382) fronted by verandas flanked by staircases. Villas to the southern end (Nos. 507–9) indicate that this was the seafront before land reclamation. Turn left to the Katong Antique House (open by appointment), at No. 208, or right into East Coast Road.

HIGHLIGHTS

- Guan Hoe Soon Restaurant
- Joo Chiat Complex
- Katong Antique House
- Koon Seng Road
- Malay Village
- Malay-style bungalows
- Old seafront luxury villas
- Peranakan-style shop-houses
- Residential terraces

INFORMATION

- ✚ L4–L5
- ✉ Joo Chiat Road
- ☎ Guan Hoe Soon 6344 2761. Katong Antique House 6345 8544
- 🍴 Guan Hoe Soon (*nonya* food, No. 214); Casa Bom Vento (No. 47); Mum's Kitchen (No. 314); AJ Tandoori's (No. 328); Lemongrass (✉ 899 East Coast Road)
- 🚇 Paya Lebar then walk
- 🚌 16, 33
- ♿ None
- 🎫 Free
- ↔ East Coast Park (➤ 48)

Bishan HDB Estate

At a Bishan hawker center

To get a feel of the Singapore you won't see in travel posters and catch a glimpse of the everyday life of most Singaporeans, take a trip to a public housing estate, where most locals live, eat, socialize and shop.

Public Housing More than 84 percent of Singapore's population lives in state-subsidized Housing and Development Board apartments known as HDBs. Hundreds of these government-built blocks exist in any given area, each a small town in its own right. Bishan, developed in the early 1990s, adds to the steadily growing list of these distinctive housing estates.

See how most locals live As with most HDB areas, Bishan has its own MRT station, around which a shopping and entertainment complex, Junction 8, has been built. Wander around Junction 8's central area close to the MRT station, up Bishan Road, and from there turn right in front of the MRT, then left into Street 22. You'll come upon one of the many smaller satellite community areas, complete with its own shops and hawker center at the base of the housing blocks. On the outskirts of Bishan, at Bright Hill Drive, is Phor Kark See, a huge Buddhist temple overlooking Bishan Park.

When to visit The best times to visit are in early morning, when housewives are out shopping, and in early evening, when families get together to shop and have their evening meal at the hawker center. Try a steamboat meat—fish, meat and vegetables that diners cook in pots of boiling broth at their table—either at a hawker center or at 3rd Mini Steamboat Delight near Bishan bus interchange behind the main shopping complex.

SINGAPORE's
best

Modern Architecture

GOING UP!

Don't miss the ride in the high-speed lift of the Swissôtel the Stamford—the only way to get to the top of its 73 floors. A matter of seconds after leaving the ground floor you are deposited 741ft (226m) in the air.

The Ritz-Carlton Millenia Hotel

THE GALLERY HOTEL (2000)

Singapore's post-modern designer hip hotel on the Singapore riverside has an eye-catchingly bright exterior, transparent sides and some striking funky furnishings.

➕ D7 ✉ 76 Robertson Quay ☎ 6849 8686 🚇 Raffles Place 🍴 Three restaurants ✋ Free

THE GATEWAY (1990)

The twin towers of this office development—37 floors of darkly tinted glass—dominate this area between Ophir Road and Rochor Canal Road. The structure, with a distinctive gap in the middle, was loosely inspired by traditional Balinese split gates.

➕ F6 ✉ 152 Beach Road 🚇 City Hall ✋ Free

RITZ-CARLTON MILLENIA HOTEL (1995)

Singapore's most stylish 22-floor high luxury hotel is built on reclaimed land in Marina Bay. The glass-domed roof of the lobby is a key feature, and the grandeur understated.

➕ F7 ✉ 7 Raffles Avenue ☎ 6337 8888 🍴 Six restaurants 🚇 Raffles City ✋ Free

SINGAPORE MARRIOTT (1982)

This 33-floor hotel is rare among modern buildings, with its octagonal structure and fanciful pagoda-style roof. Its unusual appearance makes it a striking local landmark.

➕ C5 ✉ 320 Orchard Road ☎ 6735 8967 🍴 Four restaurants 🚇 Orchard ♿ Free

SUNTEC CITY (1995)

Singapore International Convention and Exhibition Centre, in Suntec City along Temasek Boulevard, built according to *feng shui* principles, alongside office towers, and with the world's largest fountain.

➕ F7 ✉ 3 Temasek Boulevard ☎ 6337 3803 🕐 Daily 10–10 🍴 Numerous restaurants 🚇 City Hall ♿ Free

SWISSÔTEL THE STAMFORD (1985)

At 741ft (226m with 73 floors), this is one of the world's tallest hotels. The Compass Rose Bar and Restaurant. at the top, allows fantastic views over much of the island.

➕ F7 ✉ 2 Stamford Road, Raffles City ☎ 6338 8585 🍴 Seven restaurants 🚇 City Hall ♿ Free

UOB PLAZA (1996)

The 66-story UOB Plaza building at the bottom of Boat Quay is impressively out of scale with the small shophouses along the river. At 918ft (280m), it is as high as Singapore building regulations allow.

➕ dll; E8 ✉ 80 Raffles Place, UOB Plaza 1 ☎ 6533 9898 🍴 Top of the Plaza Cantonese restaurant 🚇 Raffles Place ♿ Free

GOING OUTWARDS

The northern loop of Singapore's state-of-the-art metro system, the mass rapid transit (MRT), was completed in 1987. An ambitious five-year project to build the North-East Line, which links the World Trade Centre with Punggol, was completed in 2003.

The 66-story UOB Plaza

Colonial Style

WATERING HOLES

Try the Somerset Bar in the Swissôtel the Stamford hotel for evening drinks and live jazz. Alternatively, there is the fabled Long Bar at Raffles, where, amazingly in litter-free Singapore, the tradition is to throw your empty peanut shells on the floor.

In the Top 25

1 RAFFLES HOTEL (➤ 26)
12 THE PADANG (➤ 37)

CHIJMES

Chijmes started life as a convent, girls' school and orphanage in 1854. The convent closed in 1983 and the buildings were developed in the mid-1990s to house shops, bars and restaurants. The chapel is now called Chijmes Hall and is well worth a visit.

➕ E6 ✉ 30 Victoria Street 🚇 City Hall 🏷 Free

COLONIAL RESIDENCES

A walk along Cluny, Lermit and Nassim roads, between the west end of Orchard Road and the Botanic Gardens, will give glimpses of 19th-century colonial residences. These mansions come equipped for making living in the tropical heat as tolerable as possible: enormous blinds, shaded balconies and verandas, and rich, landscaped gardens.

➕ A5–B5 ✉ Cluny, Lermit and Nassim roads 🚇 Orchard 🏷 Free

GOODWOOD PARK HOTEL

This building, erected in 1900, started life as the Teutonia Club for Singapore's German population. Although there have been many alterations, the façade has remained unchanged with its pretty turrets. It was converted into a hotel after World War II.

➕ C5 ✉ 22 Scotts Road ☎ 6737 7411 🍴 Eight restaurants 🚇 Orchard 🏷 Free

POLO CLUB

Although the Polo Club is a little way out of town, its veranda makes a pleasant place for enjoying a sundowner and dinner as the light fades over the polo field (rapidly in the tropics). Worth a visit especially as non-members are allowed entry to the bar and the restaurant.

➕ D2 ✉ 80 Mount Pleasant Road ☎ 6256 4530 🕐 Daily 8–11 🍴 Restaurant, bar 🚌 54, 130, 132, 156, 166 🏷 Free

Action at the Singapore Polo Club

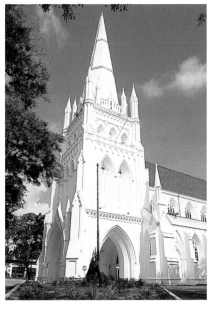

The starkly white, Gothic-style St. Andrew's Cathedral

RAFFLES HOTEL—BILLIARDS

Billiards was a popular sport in colonial times. The famed Bar and Billiards Room at Raffles Hotel houses a 100-year-old table (under which a tiger is said to have once been seen) and also serves the famous Singapore Sling—an excellent way to unwind after a day of sightseeing.

➕ F6 ✉ 1 Beach Road ☎ 6337 1886 🍴 Several restaurants (➤ 26) 🕐 Sun–Thu 11am–1am, Fri, Sat 6pm–2am 🚇 City Hall

RAFFLES HOTEL—TIFFIN

Tiffin is the light meal originally taken at midday by colonial officials in India; a mixture of English and Asian fare was usually served. Today the delicious tiffin buffet available at lunch and dinner in the Tiffin Room of the Raffles Hotel recalls the colonial custom.

➕ F6 ✉ 1 Beach Road ☎ 6337 1886 🍴 Several restaurants (➤ 26) 🕐 Tiffin served daily noon–2 and 7–10 🚇 City Hall

ST. ANDREW'S CATHEDRAL

Completed in 1861, St. Andrew's was the focus of Anglican religious life during colonial times and is still a popular place of worship. It was built by convict Indian labor and the whiter-than-white exterior is said to have been achieved by the use of Madras *chunan*—a mixture of shell lime, egg white and sugar—commonly used in India.

➕ E7 ✉ St. Andrew's Road ☎ 6337 6104 🕐 Daily 8–6 🚇 City Hall 🎫 Free

55

Museums & Places of Worship

DRAGONS

Dragons are a common symbol in Chinese temples, and represent the opposing forces of *yin* and *yang*. In Thian Hock Keng Temple (➤ 28), they can be seen on the roof ridges and the huge granite pillars near the entrance.

Gold dragon in Thian Hock Keng Temple

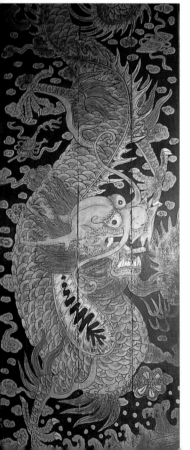

MUSEUMS

FUK TAK CHI MUSEUM

This was the first Chinese temple in Singapore. The temple originally stood right on the waterfront. Newly arrived Chinese immigrants would hop off their boat after a long hard voyage and go straight into the temple to thank the gods for a safe passage, and to ask for prosperity in business. Thanks to land reclamation, it now stands in the middle of Far East Square on the edge of the financial district.

➕ cII; E8 ✉ Telok Ayer Street ☎ 6227 7531 (Far East Square) 🚇 Raffles Place 🎟 Free

ISTANA BESAR

In neighboring Johor Bahru, the Sultan's Palace is now a fascinating museum that traces the history of the local royal family. You can visit the throne room, the family bedrooms and banquet halls and view many displays.

➕ Off map to north ✉ Jalan Ayer Molek ☎ 6223 0555 🕐 Sat–Thu 10–5 🚌 170 🎟 Moderate

RAFFLES MUSEUM

This charming small museum was set up when the hotel re-opened after renovation in 1991. Artifacts and memorabilia associated with the hotel were gathered together from its own collection and by advertising. The result is a delightful display of early plans and photographs, personal letters and postcards (some from well-known guests), luggage labels, travel posters and the like.

➕ F6 ✉ Raffles Hotel Arcade ☎ 6337 1886 🕐 Daily 10–7 🍴 Many nearby in Raffles Hotel and Raffles City 🚇 City Hall 🎟 Free

PLACES OF WORSHIP

ARMENIAN CHURCH

The Church of St. Gregory the Illuminator was built in 1835 for the small Armenian community that even at this early date had already been attracted to the growing port of Singapore. It has the distinction of being the oldest surviving Christian church in Singapore, and is still used as a place of worship. There are occasional services, and times are posted on the notice board at the entrance.

➕ E7 ✉ 60 Hill Street ☎ 6334 0141 🕒 Daily 8–8 🚇 City Hall 💵 Free

CHETTIAR TEMPLE

The temple of Sri Thandayuthanapani, rebuilt in 1984, is also called Chettiar Temple after the Indian *chettiars* (moneylenders) who financed its construction in the 1850s. The *gopuram* is a riot of images and colors. Each glass panel of the unusual 48-panel ceiling frieze, brought from India, features a deity from the Hindu pantheon.

➕ D6 ✉ 15 Tank Road ☎ 6737 9393 🕒 Daily 8–noon, 5.30–8.30 🚇 Dhoby Ghaut 💵 Free

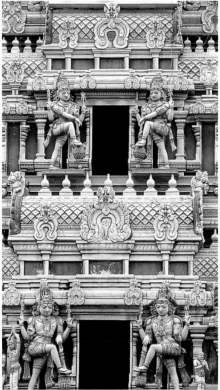

Detail of the gopuram *of Chettiar Temple*

NAGORE DURGHA SHRINE

This undeniably picturesque small mosque close to Thian Hock Keng Temple was built around 1820 for the Indian Muslim community by Chulias, southern Indian Muslims from the Coromandel Coast. Painted in white and green, it has tiny minarets and a facade of small archways and delicate plaster grilles.

➕ cII; E8 ✉ 140 Telok Ayer Street ☎ 6324 0021 🕒 Daily 10–10 🚇 Raffles Place 💵 Free

SRI SRINIVASA PERUMAL TEMPLE

Like many of the Hindu temples in Singapore, this temple has a *gopuram*, a main worshipping hall, and a shrine for the gods. The *gopuram* was built in 1979, funded by a leading Singapore merchant, P. Govindasamy Pillai, whose name also appears over one or two of the shops in Little India.

➕ F4 ✉ Serangoon Road ☎ 6298 5771 🕒 Daily 6–noon, 6–9 🚇 Bugis 💵 Free

SINGAPORE'S NATIONAL FLOWER

The orchid *Vanda* "Miss Joaquim"–a natural hybrid–is named after Agnes Joaquim, a Dutch expatriate, who discovered it one morning in 1893 growing in her garden. She is buried in the small graveyard of the Armenian Church (► 56).

57

Gardens & Green Spaces

WHAT'S IN A NAME?

The Chinese Garden is full of romantically named sites: Cloud-Piercing Pagoda, Courtyard of Early Spring, Moon Inviting Boat and Tiger's Roar Waterfall. With romance in the air, the gardens are popular with young couples as a backdrop for wedding photographs.

CHINATOWN AND TANJONG PAGAR

If you feel like a little tranquility after the hustle and bustle of Chinatown, find the path (backing Bukit Pasoh and Craig roads) that runs between New Bridge Road, opposite Pearl Centre, and Tanjong Pagar. Shady trees and handy benches line the route, which takes you past renovated shophouses and a Buddhist temple and brings you out at Tanjong Pagar food center.

🚇 bIII; D8 ✉ Bukit Pasoh and Craig roads

CHINESE AND JAPANESE GARDENS

Chinese and Japanese classical gardens have been created on two islands in Jurong Lake. The Chinese Garden covers 32 acres (13ha) and is dotted with pagodas, pavilions and arched bridges. The main building is based on Beijing's Summer Palace. During the mid-autumn festival the gardens are hung with lanterns. The Japanese Gardens are altogether more serene, and take their inspiration from gardens of the 15th to 17th centuries.

🚇 Off map to west ✉ 1 Chinese Garden Road ☎ 6264 3455
🕐 Daily 9–6.30 🍴 Refreshment kiosks 🚉 Chinese Garden
💲 Inexpensive

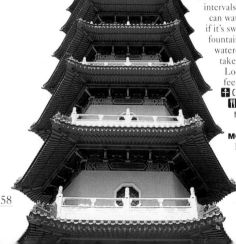

A pagoda in the Chinese Garden

MACRITCHIE RESERVOIR PARK

You can jog or walk on the shaded paths around the reservoir's edge; there are exercise stations at intervals. From the bridge you can watch turtles and carp and, if it's switched on, you'll see the fountain, which features 30 water-jet patterns. Concerts take place in the pavilion. Look for monkeys, but don't feed them.

🚇 C1 ✉ Lornie Road 🕐 24 hours
🍴 Food kiosk 🚉 MRT to Newton
then bus 104, 132 or 167 💲 Free

MOUNT FABER PARK

Rewarding views of Keppel Harbour, Sentosa Island and, on clear days, some of the Indonesian Riau Islands can be seen from the top of Mount Faber, a signal station in the 19th century. The park's 180 acres (73ha) have been planted with a variety of trees and shrubs; the bougainvillea, which flower year-round in Southeast Asia, particularly stand out. A cable car connects the top of Mount Faber to the World Trade Centre (WTC) and Sentosa Island.

➕ B9 ✉ Mount Faber Road 🕐 24 hours 🍴 Café 🚇 MRT to City Hall then bus 61, 124, 143 or 166 🎟 Free

PASIR RIS PARK
This 175-acre (71-ha) area contains some of Singapore's last remaining stretches of mangrove swamp, and is now a bird and nature reserve. Raised boardwalks meander through this habitat. Look for fiddler crabs, mudskippers and small-clawed otters. Birds you might spot include herons, yellow-vented bulbuls, brown-throated sunbirds and collared kingfishers. The best way to explore is by bicycle and there are a couple of places that rent out moutain bicycles.

➕ Off map to northeast ✉ Off Jalan Loyang Kecil 🕐 24 hours 🚇 MRT to Pasir Ris then bus 403 🎟 Free

PULAU UBIN ISLAND
This island is situated just off the northeastern corner of the mainland and consists of 2,520 acres (1,020ha) of coconut and abandoned rubber plantations, old granite quarries and mangrove swamps. Shaded trails through forest offer good bird sightings. You can rent a bicycle, dine on local seafood and generally experience *kampung* life that has long vanished from mainland Singapore.

➕ Off map to northeast 🚇 MRT to Tanah Merah then bus 2 to Changi Village, then 10-minute bumboat ride from Changi Jetty to Pulau Ubin 🎟 Ferry tickets moderate

SUNGEI BULOH NATURE RESERVE (► 21)

St. John's Island

MANGROVES—UNIQUE ADAPTATIONS
Mangrove plants have adapted to salty, swampy conditions. Some species have "breathing roots," called pneumatophores, others a tangle of aerial roots. These allow the plant to take in more oxygen, which helps it eliminate the salt absorbed from the water. You can see mangroves at Sungei Buloh and Pasir Ris reserves.

59

Parascending is just one of the many sports possible in Singapore

Outdoor Activities

ARCHERY

ARCHERY TRAINING CENTRE

The only place for archery aficionados and anyone wishing to take up the sport. It has a range that allows shooting up to 230ft (70m).

➕ D2 ✉ Singapore Polo Club, 80 Mount Pleasant Road ☎ 6256 4530 🕐 Daily 9–6 🚌 160, 166, 167, 605, 851 💲 Expensive. Courses charged for six lessons

BICYCLE RENTAL

SDK RECREATION

Bicycle rental is available near the East Coast Recreation Centre, and one of many kiosks along the 2-mile (3-km) East Coast Parkway cycle track.

➕ Off map to east ✉ 1000 East Coast Parkway, #01-00 ☎ 6445 2969/6241 5214 🕐 Mon–Fri 10–8, Sat 9–8, pub hols 8–8 🍴 Cafés and restaurants nearby 🚇 Bedok then bus 401; Eunos then bus 55 or 155 💲 Moderate

CLIMBING

CLIMB ASIA

A full equipped climbing center with two levels of climbing surfaces, a two-story vertical wall and a well-stocked climbing store.

➕ E4 ✉ 117 Rangoon Road ☎ 6292 7701 🕐 Mon 5pm–11pm, Tue–Sun 10am–11pm 🚇 Farrer Park (Exit B) then bus 131

FLYING

REPUBLIC OF SINGAPORE FLYING CLUB

Plane rental and lessons are available. If it's panoramic aerial views you're after, ask about sightseeing flights.

➕ Off map to north ✉ Seletar Air Base, Building 140B, East Camp ☎ 6481 0200 🕐 Daily 9–5.30 🚇 Yio Chu Kang then bus 59, 214E 💲 Expensive

GOLF

LAGUNA NATIONAL GOLF & COUNTRY CLUB

This club has two full golf courses: a 7,115 yard, par 73; and a 6,794 yard, par 72. There is also a 600 yard, par 54 putting course with 18 holes. Amenities include a swimming pool, children's playground and playroom, tennis, billiards and a gymnasium. Saturday is members only, but there's sometimes a free slot.

➕ Off map to east ✉ 11 Laguna Golf Green ☎ 6541 0289 🕐 Daily 7–7 🍴 Restaurant, café 🚇 Tanah Merah 💲 Expensive

A DAY OUT ON THE FAIRWAY

The Laguna Club has probably the most extensive golf facilities in Singapore, and possibly in Asia. It has two championship 18-hole courses designed by Andy Dye, a driving range and a chipping green, all beautifully landscaped on reclaimed land. The resort's facilities, centered around the clubhouse, make for a pleasant day out even for non-golfing friends and family members.

SELETAR COUNTRY CLUB

This is one of the handful of country clubs open to non-Singapore residents on weekends. It features a nine-hole, 3,156 yard, par 35 course beside Seletar Reservoir in the north of the island.

🔟 Off map to north ✉ 101 Seletar Club Road ☎ 6481 4812
🕐 Daily 9–10 🍴 Restaurant 🚌 59, 103 or 163, then 214
💲 Expensive

SCUBA DIVING

MARSDEN BROTHERS

Marsden Bros have the only custom-made dive boat in Singapore and offer excellent PADI (Professional Association of Diving Instructors) dive courses. They run to Singapore's southern reefs around Pulau Hantu and Pulau Salu.

🔟 Off map to west ✉ 113 Holland Road (by Farrer Road flyover)
☎ 6475 0050 🚌 5, 7, 61, 75, 77, 105, 106, 123, 156, 165, 174, 200 💲 Expensive

SENTOSA WATER SPORTS CENTRE

Dive trips, day-trips, lessons, and diving equipment sales and rentals. Equipment for a variety of other watersports is also available for rental.

🔟 B10 ✉ 1 Maritime Square, #01-06, Harbourfront Centre
☎ 6274 5612 🕐 Daily 9–7 🍴 Various outlets in Harbourfront Centre 🚇 (➤ 34) 💲 Expensive

TENNIS

SINGAPORE TENNIS CENTRE

Courts open to the public for day and evening play. Rackets and balls for rent and lessons available. Take a taxi there.

🔟 N6 ✉ East Coast Parkway ☎ 6442 5966 🕐 Daily 9am–11pm 💲 Moderate

WINDSURFING & SAILING

EUROPA SAILING CLUB

Basic equipment can be rented here and lessons are also available. The club has a bar, shop and café. You can join a beach barbecues on Sunday and Wednesday evenings.

🔟 Off map to east ✉ East Coast Sailing Lagoon, 1212 East Coast Parkway
☎ 6449 5118 🕐 Daily 10–5 (café closed Mon) 🍴 Café, restaurant, barbecues 🚌 Bedok then bus 31 or 197 💲 Moderate

TAKING TO THE WATERS

With the Riau Islands and the ships in the strait seaward, and the palm-fringed East Coast Park backed by luxury condominiums landward, sailing from the East Coast offers spectacular views. Winds are often best in mid-afternoon, but currents can be strong. The best days end when you come ashore to a barbecue on the beach and the music of a live band.

Watersports are popular in the warm seas around Singapore

For Children

RING OF FIRE

Although it lies very close to some of the world's most active volcanoes (in Indonesia), Singapore itself has no volcanic activity. Not, that is, until 1994, when an active volcano miraculously appeared on an island just south of Singapore—part of VolcanoLand, an attraction on Sentosa (▶ 34). Not to worry, it poses no hazard despite "erupting" every 30 minutes.

BORDERS BOOKSHOP

Borders has a children's section with an atmosphere that encourages kids to pick up books and read on the spot. Author story-telling sessions for children are regular events—look on the notice board at the main entrance for details. There is also a restaurant and a café, and CDs as well as books.

🚇 C5 ✉ 501 Orchard Road ☎ 6235 7146 🕐 Sun–Thu 9–11; Fri, Sat 9–midnight 🍴 Café and restaurant 🚇 Orchard

HAW PAR VILLA (TIGER BALM GARDENS)

This theme park, built in 1937, is based on Chinese myth and legend and real-crimes in old Singapore. Brightly painted statues, boat rides, a 197-ft (60-m) long dragon and animated puppets will entertain children.

🚇 Off map to west ✉ 262 Pasir Panjang Road ☎ 6872 2003 🕐 Daily 9–9 🍴 Cafés 🚇 MRT Buona Vista then bus 200 🎟 Free

MING VILLAGE

Here, artist craftsmen use age-old techniques to re-create the porcelain of the Ming and Qing dynasties. You can view traditional Chinese porcelain making processes including mold-making, hand-throwing, glazing, hand-painting and firing, under a single roof. Guided tours are daily from 9am to 5.30pm, and a good selection of products is on sale.

🚇 Off map to west ✉ 32 Pandan Road, Jurong ☎ 6265 7711 🕐 Daily 9–5.30 🍴 Restaurants 🚇 MRT to Clementi then bus 78 🎟 Free

Tea-time at Singapore Zoo

UNDERWATER WORLD (SENTOSA)

In Asia's largest aquarium, a moving walkway takes you through a dome-shaped glass tunnel, while hundreds of species of the region's sea creatures swim above and around you. This is the closest many people ever get to a living coral reef. Look for the starfish, sharks, poisonous lionfish and beautiful weedy sea dragons.

🚇 Off map to south ✉ 80 Siloso Road ☎ 6275 0030 🕐 Daily 9–9 🍴 Restaurant 🚇 (▶ 34). Bus or monorail from main ferry terminal on Sentosa 🎟 Moderate

SINGAPORE
where to...

Chinese

PRICES

For dinner per person for three courses, without drinks, expect to pay appoximately:

$ up to S$20
$$ S$20–S$40
$$$ more than S$40

Note: $=Singapore dollars

HOKKIEN VARIATION ON A SPRING ROLL

Popiah – freshly prepared rice-flour pancakes filled with a mouthwatering mixture of onion, turnip, bean sprouts, minced pork and prawns, all held together with a sweet soy sauce and flavored with coriander, garlic and chili– makes a delicious snack. You can order *popiah* in some restaurants, and many hawker centers have a *popiah* stall.

STEAMBOAT

Not a form of transport, rather a delicious method of tableside cooking where a selection of fish, meat and vegetables is placed in a container of boiling broth; you can cook it to your liking and retrieve it with chopsticks when it's achieved perfect readiness.

BENG THIN HOON KEE ($$)

Hokkien food is popular in Singapore, for the ancestors of many Singaporeans lived in southern China, where the cuisine originated. Try duck in lotus leaves.
✚ dll; E7 ✉ #05-02 OCBC Building, 65 Chulia Street ☎ 6533 7708 ⏰ Daily 11–12.45, 6–9.45 Ⓜ Raffles Place

BLUE GINGER ($$)

Set in an old shophouse, this is the best place in Singapore to try Peranakan dishes such as fried port and prawn rolls, *ayam panggang* (chicken in coconut milk) and durian desserts.
✚ biv; D9 ✉ 97 Tanjong Pagar Road, Chinatown ☎ 6222 3928 ⏰ Daily 11.30–2.30, 6–10 Ⓜ Tanjong Pagar

CHARMING GARDEN ($$)

Hunan and Szechuan specialties include fried yam rolls, steamed minced pigeon and dragon bearded prawns.
✚ C4 ✉ Copthorne Orchid Singapore, 214 Dunearn Road ☎ 6251 8149 ⏰ Daily 11.30–2.30, 6.30–10.30 Ⓜ Newton

CHATTERBOX ($)

Good quality, low priced local cuisine incuding Hainanese chicken, *nasi lemak* (rice cooked in coconut milk) and *laksa* (a one-dish meal of rice noodles with seafood or chicken).
✚ C5 ✉ Mandarin Hotel, 333 Orchard Road ☎ 6737 4411 ⏰ 24 hours Ⓜ Orchard

CRYSTAL JADE ($$)

Traditional Cantonese cuisine including fresh seafood dishes, barbecued pork and soups. A real Singapore dining experience.
✚ C6 ✉ #04-19 Ngee Ann City, 391 Orchard Road ☎ 6735 2388 ⏰ Daily 11.30–2.30, 6.30–10.30 Ⓜ Orchard

IMPERIAL HERBAL RESTAURANT ($$$)

Ants and scorpions, anyone? You'll find them on the menu here.
✚ F6 ✉ Metropole Hotel, 41 Seah Street ☎ 6337 0491 ⏰ Daily 11.30–2.30, 6.30–10.30 Ⓜ City Hall

LEI GARDEN ($$$)

The CHIJMES branch of this upscale chain serves Cantonese specialties such as Beijing duck.
✚ E6 ✉ 30 Victoria Street ☎ 6339 3822 ⏰ Daily 11.30–2.30, 6–10.30 Ⓜ City Hall

WAK LOK CANTONESE RESTAURANT ($$)

Fine Cantonese dinners and tasty dim sum lunches. Hong Kong Chinese come here to eat.
✚ E6 ✉ Carlton Hotel, 76 Bras Basah Road ☎ 6311 8188 ⏰ Mon–Sat 11.30–2.30, 6–10.30; Sun 11–2.30, 6.30–10.30 Ⓜ City Hall

WEE NAM KEE ($)

Here you can get an excellent version of one of the most popular local dishes, Hainanese chicken rice—chicken meat with rice and broth.
✚ D3 ✉ 275 Thomson Road ☎ 6255 6396 ⏰ Daily 10am–2am Ⓜ Novena

Indian

ANNALAKSHMI ($$)

Excellent buffet lunches with a choice of vegetable curries. In the evening there's a tempting array of classical Indian vegetarian dishes. No prices on the menu; pay what you think is fair (suggestions provided).

✚ E7 ✉ Peninsula Excelsior Hotel, 5 Coleman Street ☎ 6339 9993 🕔 Mon–Sat 11.30–3, 6–10 🚇 City Hall

BANANA LEAF APOLLO ($$)

A southern Indian "banana-leaf" restaurant where the leaf takes the place of a plate—with a good range of dishes to accompany the vegetable curries.

✚ E5 ✉ 56 Race Course Road ☎ 6293 8682 🕔 Daily 10.30–10 🚇 Bugis

KINARA ($$)

Food from northern India is served in what looks like the inside of a Rajasthani fort. Eating here is memorable. The food is good, though helpings can be small.

✚ d!; E7 ✉ 57 Boat Quay ☎ 6533 0412 🕔 Mon–Fri 11.30–2.30, 6.30–10.30; Sat–Sun 6.30–10.45 🚇 Raffles Place

KOMALA VILAS ($)

Southern Indian fare is served here on banana leaves. It's good and inexpensive, and you can have unlimited helpings of the vegetarian food. Basic meals include vegetable curries and rice with side dishes of dhal and *dosai* (thin pancakes).

For a different drink, try the sweet, spicy *masala* tea.

✚ E5 ✉ 78 Serangoon Road ☎ 6294 5294 🕔 Daily 7am–10.30pm 🚇 Bugis

MUTHU'S CURRY HOUSE ($$)

Vegetable curries are dished out fast and furiously to accompany meat, crab, squid or fish. Try the famous fish-head curry.

✚ E5 ✉ 78 Race Course Road ☎ 6293 2389 🕔 Daily 10–10 🚇 Bugis

NIRVANA ($$)

This is the sister restaurant of the famed Moti Mahal on Murray Street, and offers a similar menu of north Indian tandoori dishes.

✚ F4 ✉ 2 Owen Road ☎ 6297 0400 🕔 Daily 11.30–2.30, 6.30–10.30 (closed Tuesday evenings) 🚇 Lavender

OUR VILLAGE ($$)

North and northwest Indian food is prepared "village style" here. Try the *handi gosht*, a lamb curry. Tasty desserts.

✚ d!; E7 ✉ 5th Floor, 46 Boat Quay ☎ 6538 3058 🕔 Daily 11.30–1.30, 6–10.30 🚇 Bugis

RANG MAHAL ($$$)

This restaurant has moved to the ultra-modern Pan Pacific Hotel but is still serving a good range of North Indian dishes and an extensive lunch and dinner buffet. Indian dancers perform.

✚ F7 ✉ #03–00 Pan Pacific Hotel, Raffles Boulevard, ☎ 6333 1788 🕔 Daily 12–2.30, 7–11 🚇 City Hall

HAND OR CUTLERY?

Many Hindus and Muslims eat their food with the right hand only; it is considered unclean to eat with the left hand, although it's okay to use utensils—usually a fork and spoon. Eating with your hand, you tear pieces of chapati (using only one hand) and then soak up or scoop up elements of the meal. For rice there's another technique: you add the curries and work up the mixure into balls which you then pick up and pop—almost flick—into your mouth.

Other Asian Fare

"SATAY! SATAY!"

No trip to Singapore would be complete without the famous *satay*, a Malay dish. Sticks of chicken, lamb or beef, and sometimes other foods such as tofu, are barbecued and served with a thick, sweet peanut sauce. Small rice cakes and cucumber usually accompany the satay. It is served in some restaurants, and at many hawker centers there is a "satay man." If you develop a taste for it, look in supermarkets for the ready-made *satay* sauce and try it at home with a barbecue.

HAE BOK'S KOREAN RESTAURANT ($$)

Reliably good Korean dishes such as fried octopus with Korean spicy sauce and fried, egg-coated vegetables.
✚ E8 ✉ 44–46 Tanjong Pagar Road ☎ 6223 9003 ⏰ Daily 11.30–3, 5.30–10.30 Ⓠ Tanjong Pagar

HOUSE OF SUNDANESE FOOD ($$)

Spicy food from west Java—the fish dishes are particularly good.
✚ E7 ✉ 77 High Street ☎ 6339 9974 ⏰ Mon–Fri 11–2, Sat 12–2.30, 6–10 Ⓠ City Hall

INAGIKU ($$$)

Some of the best Japanese food outside Tokyo. Includes sushi, tempura, sashimi and *teppanyaki* dishes. All this plus restful Japanese ambience.
✚ F6 ✉ 2 Stamford Road, The Westin Plaza, Level 3 ☎ 6431 6156 ⏰ Daily 12–3.30, 6.30–10.30 Ⓠ City Hall

INDOCHINE ($$)

This trendy renovated shophouse is a popular drinking sport for expatriates on weekdays. Vietnamese/ Cambodian/Laotian dishes include spicy sausage and deep-fried fish.
✚ cii; E8 ✉ 49 Club Street ☎ 6323 0503 ⏰ Daily 12–3, 6–10.30 Ⓠ Chinatown

NONYA AND BABA ($$)

Dishes such as *otak-otak* (fish cake in banana leaves) and *itek tim* (duck soup) are typical examples of *nonya* food (a fusion of Chinese and Malay cuisines). The rice- and coconut-based desserts are worth trying.
✚ D6 ✉ 262 River Valley Road ☎ 6734 1386 ⏰ Daily 11–3, 6–10 Ⓠ Dhoby Ghaut 🚌 32, 54, 195

PATARA ($$)

The chef here likes to try fusion cusine, which often include variations on Thai classics such as green curries, deep-fried fish and vegetable dishes.
✚ B5 ✉ #03-14 Tanglin Mall, 163 Tanglin Road ☎ 6737 0818 ⏰ Daily 12–2.30, 6–10.30 Ⓠ Orchard

SAKANA ($$)

Perfect for a low-key meal, whether for their set-price lunches or à la carte dinners.
✚ F6 ✉ #01-03/04 Liang Seah Street ☎ 6336 0266 ⏰ Mon–Sat 12–2.30, 6–10 Ⓠ City Hall

TAMBUAH MAS ($$)

Very good Indonesian food—don't miss the *ikan bilis* (whitebait and peanuts) and *soto ayam* (thick chicken soup)— almost Java's national dish. A branch is at the Shaw Centre.
✚ B5 ✉ #04-10 Tanglin Shopping Centre, 19 Tanglin Road ☎ 6733 3333 ⏰ Daily 10–11 Ⓠ Orchard

THANYING ($$)

This Thai restaurant is always packed. Try the green curries and stuffed chicken wings.
✚ E7 ✉ 3D River Valley Road, 01–14 Clarke Quay ☎ 6336 1821 ⏰ Mon–Sat 11.30–3, 6.30–11 Ⓠ City Hall

Hawker Centers

CHINA SQUARE (S)

This sprawling three-floor food complex has Western food outlets and traditional hawker fare under one roof.

🕂 cll; E8 ✉ Telok Ayer Street ⏰ Daily 7am–10pm 🚇 Raffles Place

CHINATOWN COMPLEX FOOD CENTRE (S)

Large buzzing food court in the middle of Chinatown with most types of local Chinese food available plus a range of desserts—try the ice *kacang*.

🕂 bll; D8 ✉ Chinatown Complex, Smith Street ⏰ Early till late daily 🚇 Outram Park

EAST COAST LAGOON FOOD CENTRE (S)

The good food and sea breezes make this popular. The *satay* is very good, as are the *laksa* and any number of tantalizing seafood dishes including chili or black pepper crab, and cuttlefish.

🕂 Off map to east ✉ East Coast Parkway ⏰ Late morning till late daily 🚇 Bugis, then bus 401 (Sat, Sun, hols only)

LAU PA SAT (S)

This ornate iron building, built in 1894, is the largest Victorian filigree cast-iron structure left in South East Asia. It houses many of Singapore's best hawker stalls.

🕂 diii; E8 ✉ 18 Raffles Quay ⏰ 24 hours 🚇 Raffles

MAXWELL ROAD (S)

This hawker center is nicely old-fashioned—not many bright lights or modern conveniences. The food is good, especially some of the basics like chicken rice and *murtabak*.

🕂 bll; E8 ✉ Corner of Maxwell Road and South Bridge Road ⏰ Early till late daily 🚇 Tanjong Pagar

NEWTON CIRCUS (S)

Probably the most expensive of the hawker centers, and popular with bus tours. More than 100 stalls offer every type of local food. Lobster is good, and try the carrot cake (stir-fried radish with eggs).

🕂 D5 ✉ Clemenceau Avenue ⏰ Daily 24 hours 🚇 Newton

PICNIC FOOD COURT (S)

This air-conditioned food court in the basement of Scotts shopping mall is handy when you are shopping. A variety of stalls include Korean, Thai, Indian, Japanese, Malay, steamboat and vegetarian options.

🕂 C5 ✉ Picnic Food Court, Scotts , Scotts Road ⏰ Sun–Thu 10.30–10; Fri, Sat, eve of public hols 10.30–10.30 🚇 Orchard

ZHUJIAO FOOD CENTRE (S)

A good place to watch the world go by. Get up early and have an Indian breakfast and watch it being prepared: *roti prata* (curry gravy with bread) and, to drink, *teh tarik* (aerated tea).

🕂 E5 ✉ Zhujiao Food Market, Serangoon Road ⏰ Daily early till late 🚇 Bugis

POPULAR ORDERS AT A GLANCE

Bandung Rose syrup and evaporated milk—it's the lurid pink drink!

Beef kway teow Flat noodles with beef.

Char kway teow Flat noodles with prawns, pork and beansprouts.

Chicken rice As it sounds!

Chili crab Crab, chili and tomato sauce, garlic; served in the shell.

Ice kacang Red beans, jelly, sweet corn, shaved ice and evaporated milk.

Laksa Rice noodles and prawns in coconut milk with chili.

Mee goreng Fried spicy noodles.

Murtabak Pancake with minced chicken, mutton or sardine filling.

Nasi biryani Rice and spiced chicken or mutton.

Shabu-shabu The name refers to the sound made as paper-thin beef is moved back and forth in a bubbling broth. It is cooked at the table in a copper pot.

Italian

A TASTE OF ITALY

Singaporeans and visitors alike have latched on to Italian cuisine and new Italian restaurants are springing up all the time all over Singapore. Even fast-food chains such as Pizza Hut and Milano's do well. So if you're craving something other than rice and Asian noodles, you might want to look out for fresh Italian pasta and pizzas.

AL FORNO TRATTORIA (SS)

A popular restaurant, though a little way out of the center of the city, so be sure to make a reservation. Antipasto and pizzas are particularly tasty.

➕ D3 ✉ 203 Thomson Road ☎ 6256 2838 🕐 Daily 12–2, 6.30–10.30 🚇 Novena

DA PAOLO E JUDIE (SSS)

People go here for the classic contemporary design and attentive service offering modern Italian cuisine. Seafood dishes are the specialty. There's also a bar with plenty of choice.

➕ aiii; D8 ✉ 81 Neil Road, Chinatown ☎ 6225 8306 🕐 Mon–Sat 11.30–3, 6.30–11.30 🚇 Outram Park

LA FORKETTA (SS)

Although this restaurant is a little off the beaten track it's worth the trip, as the food is delicious, particularly the first-class pizza.

➕ Off map to west ✉ 491 River Valley Road ☎ 6836 3373 🕐 Daily 12–2.30, 6–10.30 🚌 14, 32, 54, 65, 139, 195

PASTA BRAVA (SS)

A lovely restaurant in a converted shophouse on the edge of Chinatown. Some dishes can be expensive, but the food is very good. This place is popular with workers at lunch.

➕ bII; D8 ✉ 11 Craig Road ☎ 6227 7550 🕐 Daily 11–2.30, 6.30–10.30 🚇 Tanjong Pagar

PETE'S PLACE (SSS)

This basement trattoria opened in 1973 is popular with both visitors and locals. The pastas are tasty and an excellent salad bar makes the place a good bet for vegetarians. Popular for Sunday brunches.

➕ C5 ✉ Basement, Grand Hyatt Hotel, 10–12 Scotts Road ☎ 6416 7113 🕐 Daily 1.30–2.30, 6–11 🚇 Orchard

PREGO (SS)

This long-established restaurant bustles at lunch and in the evenings thanks to an excellent range of dishes and a perfect central location.

➕ E7 ✉ Westin Stamford Hotel, 2 Stamford Road ☎ 6431 5156 🕐 Daily 11.30–2.30, 6.30–10.30 🚇 City Hall

ROCKY'S (SS)

If you feel like ordering pizza to eat in, Rocky's is the place. You need to allow about an hour for delivery.

➕ Off map to west ✉ 392 Upper Bukit Timah Road ☎ 6468 9188 🕐 Daily 11–10.30 (last order 10) 🚇 No public transport

SKETCHES PASTA & WINE BAR (S)

Set around the kitchen, the idea of this friendly place is that you design your own pasta dishes from a list of fresh ingredients.

➕ F6 ✉ 200 Victoria Street, 01–85 Parco Bugis Junction ☎ 6339 8386 🕐 Daily 11–10 🚇 Bugis

Other Western Fare

BLU ($$$)

Experience fine California cuisine including such dishes as crab cakes and foie gras chicken in ultra-stylish surroundings with stunning city views.
➕ B5 ✉ Level 24, Shangri-La Hotel, 22 Orange Grove Road ☎ 6730 2598 🕐 Mon–Sat 7pm–10.30pm 🚇 Orchard

BRAZIL CHURRASCARIA ($$)

Possibly Singapore's only Brazilian eating place. Choose from the extensive, interesting set-price salad bar and then take as many as you like of the succulent spit-roasted cuts of meat brought to your table in rapid succession.
➕ Off map to west ✉ 14–16 Sixth Avenue, just off Bukit Timah Road ☎ 6463 1923 🕐 Daily 6.30pm–10.30pm 🚇 Newton then bus 156, 170, 174

ESMIRADA ($$$)

The Mediterranean/ Asian interior creates an unusual ambience but the food, from Greece, Spain, Portugal, France and Morocco, comes in generous portions.
➕ D6 ✉ 442 Orchard Road, 01–29 Orchard Hotel ☎ 6734 0782 🕐 Daily 11–11 🚇 Orchard

HARD ROCK CAFÉ ($$)

Steaks, hamburgers and huge sandwiches are the most popular items on the menu at this chain restaurant and music venue decorated with rock memorabilia.
➕ C5 ✉ #02-01 HPL House, 50 Cuscaden Road ☎ 6235 6256

🕐 Sun–Thu 7.30am–11pm, (10.30 for food) 🚇 Orchard

MARCHÉ ($)

This popular restaurant has many stands that serve dishes from all over Europe. Choose from a wonderful variety of fresh seafood and steaks, and have them cooked on the spot. Southeast Asian favorites also served.
➕ D6 ✉ 260 Orchard Road, #01-03, The Heeren ☎ 6737 6996 🕐 Daily 11–11 🚇 Somerset

MEZZA 9 ($$$)

Mezza 9 has an open kitchen with chefs working right in front of you and serving food at your table.
➕ C5 ✉ Grand Hyatt Hotel, 10/12 Scotts Road ☎ 6730 7188 🕐 Daily noon–11 🚇 Orchard

PAULANER BRÄUHAUS ($$)

German theme restaurant-cum-brewery serving generous platters of sauerkraut and *wurst kartoffeln*.
➕ F7 ✉ #01-01 Millennia Walk, 9 Raffles Boulevard ☎ 6883 2572 🕐 Daily 11.30–2.30, 6–10 (drinks only after 10) 🚇 City Hall

SEAH STREET DELI ($)

This 1950s style New York deli is perfect for lunches or light evening meals.
➕ F6 ✉ #01-22 Raffles Hotel Arcade, 1 Beach RoadMillennia Walk, 9 Raffles Boulevard ☎ 6337 1886 🕐 Sun–Thu 11–10, Fri, Sat 11–11 🚇 City Hall

DINNER IS SERVED

For a romantic evening, far from the hustle and bustle of Orchard Road or a hawker center, you can't beat the breezy hilltop terrace of Alkaff Mansion on Telok Blangah Green. It's a lovely spot for an aperitif, or a coffee after your meal. The restored salons, hung with huge mirrors upstairs and down, make for wonderful, old-fashioned dining rooms. Also don't miss the charming toilets. If you want to enjoy the terrace by day, stop by for the restaurant's delicious high tea.

Vegetarian & Do-It-Yourself

WHAT'S FOR DESSERT?

While Singapore may not be known for its apple pies and cream tortes, it does have something just as tempting—tropical fruits. Here's a rundown of favorites:

Durian This huge, spiky fruit, when opened, reveals a creamy-yellow, soft, slimy interior and smells phenomenally bad. However, if you can get used to the aroma, the taste is not unpleasant. Not for the fainthearted!

Guava Looking like huge pears, guavas usually have a pink granular flesh that is used to make a thick, sweet drink.

Rambutan This small, red, hairy fruit sold in bunches is delicious. The firm, white flesh is sweet and rather like that of a lychee.

Papaya This large, elongated fruit is traditionally served for breakfast with lime juice and is rich in vitamin A.

VEGETARIAN

FUT SAI KAI VEGETARIAN RESTAURANT ($$)

Few Chinese are vegetarians, but this unusual restaurant serves Buddhist cuisine. In addition to the many vegetables on the menu, tofu and soy bean products, often shaped to resemble meat or fish, are a specialty.

➕ F5 ✉ 147 Kitchener Road ☎ 6291 2350 🕐 Daily 10–9 🚇 Bugis

LINGZHI VEGETARIAN RESTAURANT ($)

This restaurant has an eat-in area designed like a Chinese courtyard, and a busy takeout counter. Popular dishes such as braised spinach, barbecued mushrooms and braised beancurd skin roll disappear quickly at this well-patronized restaurant. It all adds up an imaginative menu.

➕ C5 ✉ #05–01 Liat Towers, 541 Orchard Road ☎ 6734 3788 🕐 Daily 11.30–3.30, 6–10 🚇 Orchard

OLIO DOME ($$)

This restaurant chain serves an exciting range of salads, foccacia bread sandwiches and other snacks. Good choices for vegetarians.

➕ E6 ✉ Singapore Art Museum, 71 Bras Basah Road ☎ 6533 3266 🕐 Daily 10.30–10.30 🚇 City Hall

ORIGINAL SIN ($$)

The menu at this Mediterranean-style restaurant is completely vegetarian. The imaginative use of ingredients gives run-of-the-mill dishes a real twist.

➕ Off map to west ✉ Block 43, Jalan Merah Saga, #01-62 Chip Bee Gardens, Holland Village ☎ 6475 5605 🕐 Tue–Sun 11–2.30, 6–10.30 🚌 5, 7, 61, 106

SRI VIJAYA ($)

Modest vegetarian, banana-leaf establishment offering great value with its generous helpings of rice and vegetable accompaniments.

➕ E6 ✉ 229 Selegie Road ☎ 6336 1748 🕐 Daily 7am–10pm 🚇 Bugis

SUPERNATURE ($$)

Soy burgers, healthy sandwiches and fresh juices are the staples at this chic organic shop. Vegans well catered for.

➕ B6 ✉ #01–21 Park House, 21 Orchard Boulevard ☎ 6735 4338 🕐 Mon–Sat 10–8 🚇 Orchard

DO-IT-YOURSELF

If you want provisions for a picnic, check out these supermarkets.

COLD STORAGE CENTREPOINT

➕ D6 ✉ #B1-14 Centrepoint, 176 Orchard Road ☎ 6737 4222 🕐 Daily 9am–10pm 🚇 Somerset

JASON'S SUPERMARKET

➕ C5 ✉ 1 Claymore Drive, #01-01 Orchard Towers ☎ 6235 4355 🕐 Mon–Thu & Sat 8am–9pm, Fri 8am–10.30pm, Sun 9–9 🚇 Orchard

Coffee & Tea

AH TENG'S BAKERY ($)

This café in Raffles Hotel Arcade sells breads, cakes and ice-creams. Try the giant whole grain muffins—a meal in themselves.

⊞ F6 ✉ 1 Beach Road
☎ 6331 1711 ⏰ Daily
7.30am–11pm ⓂCity Hall

COFFEE CLUB, HOLLAND VILLAGE ($)

The Coffee Club specializes in interesting coffees, some with cream and a choice of different spirits.

⊞ Off the map to west ✉ 48 Lorong Mambong ☎ 6466 0296
⏰ Daily 10am–11pm 🚌 5, 7, 61, 106

DELIFRANCE ($)

One of a growing chain of cafés, this serves filled baguettes and other savories and tempting sweets.

⊞ E7 ✉ #01-03, 11 Stamford Road ☎ 6334 1645 ⏰ Daily
7.30am–10pm ⓂCity Hall

GOODWOOD PARK HOTEL ($$)

Tea is served in a light and airy dining room overlooking the hotel pool. A pianist lends a musical note.

⊞ C5 ✉ 22 Scotts Road
☎ 6737 7411 ⏰ Daily
12.30–5.30 ⓂOrchard

HILTON SINGAPORE ($$)

The Hilton clearly has a number of first-rate pastry chefs; the cake selection at teatime is a delight. Do not miss the special cheesecakes.

⊞ C5 ✉ 581 Orchard Road
☎ 6737 2233 ⏰ 12–5.30 Sat only ⓂOrchard

RAFFLES HOTEL ($$)

A sumptuous tea is served in the Tiffin Room and the Bar and Billiard restaurant. Arrive early for afternoon tea, especially at weekends.

⊞ F6 ✉ 1 Beach Road
☎ 6337 1886 ⏰ Daily
3.30–5 ⓂCity Hall

WESTERN-STYLE COFFEE OUTLETS

Singapore has many Western coffee outlets. Some of the best for people-watching are on Orchard Road.

STARBUCKS ($)

The Seattle-based chain serves high-quality coffee and iced confections along with a small selection of good-quality pastries and cakes.

⊞ E6 ✉ 68 Orchard Road, #01-34 Plaza Singapura
☎ 6837 0501 ⏰ Daily 10–10
ⓂDhoby Ghant

Also at:

⊞ C5 ✉ Orchard Point, 160 Orchard Road ☎ 6738 6940
⏰ Sun–Thu 7.30am–11am, Fri, Sat 7.30am–midnight
ⓂSomerset

SPINELLI'S ($)

⊞ D6 ✉ Heeren Building, 260 Orchard Road ☎ 6738 0233
⏰ Mon–Thu 7.30–10pm, Fri, Sat 7.30am–midnight, Sun 9am–10pm ⓂSomerset

THE COFFEE BEAN & TEA LEAF ($)

⊞ C5 ✉ #01-04/05 The Promenade, Orchard Road
☎ 6734 0090 ⏰ Sun–Thu 8am–10.30pm, Fri, Sat 8am–1am ⓂOrchard

COFFEE SHOPS

Singapore's traditional coffee shops are nothing like the modern places that sell a sophisticated selection of Javanese coffee and brownies. They are no-nonsense, cheap and cheerful options for popular local rice and noodle dishes. You also get coffee, but it's thick and sweet, made with condensed milk. Mindful of waste, coffee shops sometimes serve takeout coffee in empty condensed-milk cans, and you will occasionally see people carrying these, though the more usual coffee container today is the familiar Styrofoam container or a plastic bag, which you can sometimes see tied to railings while the contents cool.

Orchard Road West

CHANGING TIMES

"Beyond the bazaar, ... Orchard Road becomes a straight, well-shaded drive, leading to the European residences in the Tanglin district. On the left, almost hidden by the trees is a very large Chinese Burial Ground formerly used by the Teo Chews, ie Chinese hailing from Swatow. The visitor may perhaps overtake a funeral on its way to one of these Chinese burying grounds in the suburbs, with the customary accompaniments of gongs to startle, and the scattering of gold and silver paper to appease the spirit of the deceased. Orchard Road ends at the entrance to the Military Barracks in Tanglin Road."

– The Revd G. M. Reith, *Handbook to Singapore*, 1907, OUP.

TANGLIN MALL

This shopping mall provides something a little different from the designer labels on offer elsewhere on Orchard Road. The range of stores includes some interesting children's shops, a sports shop and three floors of Food Junction. A handicrafts market is held the third Saturday of every month.

✚ B5 ✉ 163 Tanglin Road ☎ 6736 4922 🕐 Daily 10–10 🚇 Orchard

TANGLIN SHOPPING CENTRE

One of the area's oldest shopping malls, this is well known for its Asian antiques and curios (though, as elsewhere in Singapore, prices are high). It is also good for carpets, tailoring and cameras and accessories. Near the intersection of Tanglin and Orchard roads.

✚ B5 ✉ 19 Tanglin Road ☎ 6732 8751 🕐 Daily 10–6 🚇 Orchard

ORCHARD TOWERS

Many small specialist traders fill this center, known particularly for its jewelry and silk shops. There are also a number of restaurants on the upper floors.

✚ C5 ✉ 400 Orchard Road 🕐 Daily 9.30am–10pm 🚇 Orchard

WHEELOCK PLACE

This striking and ideally located center is very popular. A Borders bookshop takes up much of the ground floor and is open longer hours than other shops. Marks & Spencer has the basement. There's also an organic food shop.

✚ C5 ✉ 501 Orchard Road 🕐 Sun–Thu 10.30–8.30, Fri, Sat 10.30–9.30 🚇 Orchard

SHAW CENTRE

This office-cum-small-shops center is linked to Shaw House (see below) and has a number of interesting outlets, including a reasonably priced shoe shop (Fairlady), a small clothes shop (Solo), a number of gift shops and a hardware shop (Handyman Centre).

✚ C5 ✉ 1 Scotts Road ☎ 6737 9080 🕐 Daily 10–7 🚇 Orchard

SHAW HOUSE

This is a very useful shopping mall with a supermarket and inexpensive cafés in the basement, a top-floor cinema and a well-stocked department store.

✚ C5 ✉ 350 Orchard Road ☎ 6235 1150 🕐 Daily 10–10 🚇 Orchard

PACIFIC PLAZA

Pacific Plaza is another trendy place popular with Singapore youth. They seem to line up for hours to get into Venom, a nightclub in the complex. Tower Records and Books fills two floors with books, music and magazines.

✚ C5 ✉ 9 Scotts Road ☎ 6733 5655 🕐 Daily 10–10 🚇 Orchard

Orchard Road East

FAR EAST PLAZA
More than 800 outlets offering almost everything, from clothes to haircuts, CDs and software to shoe repairs.
➕ C5 ✉ 14 Scotts Road
☎ 6734 2325 🕐 Daily 10–9
🚇 Orchard

SCOTTS
This relatively small center is very good for fashion items. With the Picnic Food Court in the basement and a SISTIC (Singapore Indoor Stadium Ticketing) counter for theater tickets, it's a handy emporium.
➕ C5 ✉ 6 Scotts Road
☎ 6734 7560 🕐 Daily 10–9 (food court 11–10) 🚇 Orchard

TANGS
Conveniently situated above Orchard MRT, this is Singapore's most famed department store and is a useful meeting point. Good for gift shopping.
➕ C5 ✉ 320 Orchard Road
☎ 6737 5500 🕐 Mon–Fri 11–9, Sat 11–9.30, Sun 12.30–8 🚇 Orchard

LUCKY PLAZA
Another huge shopping complex, full of small shops selling all manner of goods. Salespeople may be aggressive, so bargain hard.
➕ C5 ✉ 304 Orchard Road
☎ 6235 3294 🕐 Daily 10–9
🚇 Orchard

NGEE ANN CITY (► 32)

THE HEEREN
Popular among the hip and trendy. Browse the three floors of HMV or sip coffee at Spinelli's outdoor café.
➕ D6 ✉ 260 Orchard Road
☎ 6733 4725 🕐 Daily 10am–11pm 🚇 Somerset

SPECIALISTS' SHOPPING CENTRE
One of Singapore's older shopping centers, named for the doctors who have offices there. This offers a number of boutiques as well as the John Little department store and a SISTIC ticket outlet.
➕ D6 ✉ 277 Orchard Road
☎ 6737 8222 🕐 Daily 10.30–8.30 🚇 Somerset

CENTREPOINT
One of the most user-friendly complexes, with good department stores (Robinson's and Marks & Spencer) and shops selling everything from books to clothes and electrical goods, plus restaurants and a supermarket.
➕ D6 ✉ 176 Orchard Road
☎ 6235 6629 🕐 Daily 10.30–9.30 🚇 Somerset

CUPPAGE TERRACE
A pleasant change from large, glitzier shopping centers, Cuppage Terrace offers a small selection of arts and crafts shops.
➕ D6 ✉ 55 Cuppage Road
🕐 Daily 10–7 🚇 Somerset

PLAZA SINGAPURA
Boutiques, eateries, a few department stores and cinema.
➕ E6 ✉ 68 Orchard Road
☎ 6332 9298 🕐 Daily 11–9
🚇 Dhoby Ghaut

EMERALD HILL ROAD
(➕ D5–D6)
Originally a nutmeg plantation, Emerald Hill Road features magnificent Peranakan residences, built by wealthy Straits-born Teochew Chinese. Pronounced a preservation area in 1981, it has 112 terrace houses erected from 1902 to 1930. Despite being designed by 13 different architects, the streetscape is an aesthetic blend of richly detailed town houses. To get there, walk up the side road through Peranakan Place on Orchard Road. The stretch just above Peranakan Place also offers a few watering holes, including a wine bar and a beer bar.

Chinatown & the Singapore River

BARGAINING

Many Singapore shopkeepers are happy for you to bargain with them and it can save you a significant percentage, even on fairly small purchases. Don't make your first offer until the seller has reduced the opening price at least once. It is considered a matter of honor that once you have settled on a price, you must go through with the deal. Don't bargain if you see "Fixed price" signs.

HONG BAO

You may notice small red packets on sale. These *hong bao*, as they are known, are used for giving gifts of money, particularly for weddings and at Chinese New Year, when it is the custom for unmarried children to receive a red packet. Many employers also choose this time of year to give their red packets—bonuses.

CHINATOWN POINT

One of Chinatown's earliest shopping centers, containing a variety of shops and eateries, and specialising in local handicraft and gift shops.

🚇 bll; D8 ✉ 133 New Bridge Road ☎ 6534 0112 🕓 Daily 10–10 🚉 Outram Park

CLARKE QUAY & RIVERSIDE POINT (➤ 40)

This area is gaining a reputation as a bargain haunt with its Sunday flea market and over 80 shops selling everything from curios to designer wear. Adjacent to Clarke Quay is Liang Court and Robertson walk.

🚇 bl; E7 ✉ 3 River Valley Road ☎ 6227 8001 🚉 Raffles Place

GREAT WORLD CITY

Top tenants in this sprawling complex include OG and Ethan Allen. A stone's throw from Orchard Road, the complex provides a free shuttle bus from Lucky Plaza and the Paragon, and there is a variety of eateries.

🚇 C6 ✉ Kim Seng Promenade ☎ 6839 7950 🕓 Daily 10–10 🚌 16

PEOPLE'S PARK COMPLEX

You can buy all manner of goods at this bustling complex in the heart of Chinatown including traditional remedies and Asian textiles. There are plenty of clothing and electronic shops, too. This is one of the city's oldest shopping centers.

🚇 bll; D8 ✉ 1 Park Road ☎ 6535 9533 🕓 Daily 10–9.30 🚉 Outram Park

PIDEMCO CENTRE

The Pidemco Centre, home of the Singapore Jewellery Mart, is a good starting point to get an overview of the range and cost of jewelry available here.

🚇 cl; E7 ✉ 95 South Bridge Road 🕓 Mon–Sat 10.30–6 🚉 City Hall

TEMPLE/PAGODA/ TRENGGANU STREETS

In the streets between South Bridge Road and New Bridge Road, in the heart of Chinatown, shops and stalls sell a tantalizing range of Chinese goods: herbal remedies, porcelain, exotic fruit and gold jewelry. The rich smell of a Chinese favorite, barbecued pork, pervades the streets.

🚇 bll; E8 ✉ Temple Street off South Bridge Road 🚉 Outram Park

YUE HWA CHINESE PRODUCTS EMPORIUM

This well laid-out department store in the heart of Chinatown has an extensive array of quality merchandise, from traditional and modern clothes to handicrafts, food and household items.

🚇 bll; D8 ✉ 70 Eu Tong Sen Street ☎ 6538 4222 🕓 Mon–Thu 11–9.30, Fri–Sun 11–10 🚉 Outram Park

Arab Street & Little India

ALBERT STREET

Start at the Albert Complex and work your way to Albert Court (the Selegie Road end), where two rows of renovated shophouses now contain gift shops and eateries. Side streets lead to still other stands.

➕ E5 🚇 Bugis

ARAB STREET

Good handicrafts from all over Asia can be bought near the intersection of Beach Road and Arab Street, where some of the neighborhood's original shops still survive. Look for basketware, textiles, lace, silverwork, jewelry and perfume. This is the best area in Singapore for buying fabric; numerous shops offer silks, cottons and batiks.

➕ F6 ✉ Area bounded by Jalan Sultan, Beach Road, Ophir Road and Victoria Street 🚇 Bugis

DUNLOP STREET

Bursting with colorful provisions, clothing, textiles and fancy-goods shops, Dunlop Street is a microcosm of Little India. Packets of spices and Indian soaps make interesting, lightweight gifts.

➕ E5 🚇 Bugis

LITTLE INDIA ARCADE

This stretch of old shophouses has been gentrified into a rambling shopping complex. At the gateway to Little India, it has a totally Indian feel and is worth visiting for its food court and shops, which sell textiles, traditional clothing, jewelry, Indian music CDs and tapes, ayurvedic medicines, garlands and spices.

➕ E5 ✉ 48 Serangoon Road ☎ 6295 5998 🕐 Daily 9.30–9 (restaurants 9am–11pm) 🚇 Bugis

SERANGOON PLAZA

This busy emporium is always packed with Indians, Bangladeshis and others—some tourists but many locals—buying everything from food to electrical items and cosmetics. Serangoon Plaza is particularly good for cheap everyday clothes and household items.

➕ F5 ✉ 320 Serangoon Road 🕐 Mon–Thu 9.30–10, Fri–Sun 9.30–10.30 🚇 Bugis

SIM LIM SQUARE
(▶ 79)

ZHUJIAO MARKET (KK MARKET)

The ground floor of this busy market (known to Indian locals as Teka) is just the place for fruit and flowers. On the floor above the food sellers, you'll find a range of clothes, textiles, Indian handicrafts and luggage. The quality isn't the finest, but the market is a good place for bargains and unusual items—such as Chinese babywear. A food court is on the ground floor.

➕ HE5 ✉ Buffalo Road 🕐 Daily 10–7 🚇 Bugis

PERFUMERS' CORNER

At the North Bridge Road end of Arab Street, it is possible to buy perfumes made from a heady mixture of essences: attar of rose, sandalwood, jasmine, honeysuckle and other gorgeously aromatic ingredients. These come in beautiful glass bottles and, depending upon your blend, can be quite expensive. But the scents are very strong and a little goes a long way.

Handicrafts & Antiques

DAY-OLD ANTIQUES

Furniture and artifacts over 100 years old, considered antiques, are sold in a plethora of antique and reproduction shops. Buy only from reputable dealers. They will give a certificate of antiquity or a detailed description along with a receipt. This proof may be required to ensure duty-free importation to the US. Prices are usually lower in the country of origin than in Singapore; they vary widely here, and bargaining is essential.

ANTIQUES OF THE ORIENT

You could spend hours browsing through this shop's fine selection of old lithographs, prints, maps and books.
➕ B5 ✉ #02-40 Tanglin Shopping Centre, 19 Tanglin Road ☎ 6734 9351 🕐 Mon–Sat 10–6, Sun 10.30–4.30 🚇 Orchard

LAVANYA

Textiles, small carvings, traditional furniture and jewelry are among the offerings in this excellent specialty Indian shop.
➕ E7 ✉ #02-11–12 Excelsior Hotel and Shopping Centre, 5 Coleman Street ☎ 6339 9400 🕐 Mon–Sat 11.30–7 🚇 City Hall

LIM'S ARTS & CRAFTS

Authentic handicrafts, including linens, jewelry, pottery and silk pyjamas.
➕ Off map to west ✉ #02-01 Holland Road Shopping Centre, 211 Holland Avenue ☎ 6467 1300 🕐 Mon–Sat 9.30–8.30, Sun, public hols 10.30–6.30 🚌 5, 7, 61, 106

MATA-HARI

The basketry, lacquerware and silver jewelry here originate from Thailand, Cambodia, Vietnam, Indonesia and Myanmar (Burma).
➕ B5 ✉ #02-26 Tanglin Shopping Centre, 19 Tanglin Road ☎ 6737 6068 🕐 Mon–Sun 10.30–6.30 🚇 Orchard

MUSEUM SHOP

A lovely selection of Chinese ceramics and handicrafts from Southeast and South Asia—sarongs, silver jewelry, shawls and woven baskets from Lombok.
➕ E6 ✉ 53 Armenian Street ☎ 6339 2011 🕐 Tue–Sun 9.30–6.30 🚇 City Hall

PARAGON ART & ANTIQUE GALLERY

On the fifth floor of the Paragon Shopping Centre are 11 art and antique galleries selling quality Chinese paintings, porcelain, woodcarvings and sculpture. A good place to learn about Chinese fine arts.
➕ D6 ✉ Level 5, Paragon Shopping Centre, 290 Orchard Road ☎ 6738 5535 🕐 Daily 10–8 🚇 Somerset

POLAR ARTS OF ASIA

Treasures from all over Asia pack this shop. Plates and pots from Nepal, Myanmar and the Thai hill tribes, spears from Papua New Guinea and penis gourds are just a few eye-catching items.
➕ C5 ✉ #02-16 Far East Shopping Centre, Orchard Road ☎ 6734 2311 🕐 Mon–Sat 11–6 🚇 Orchard

SINGAPORE HANDICRAFT CENTRE

Five floors of shops in the heart of Chinatown, where you can find all manner of curios, including antique snuff bottles, carpets and calligraphic works.
➕ bII; D8 ✉ Chinatown Point, 133 New Bridge Road 🕐 Daily 10–10 🚇 Outram Park

Eastern Trading Goods

ALJUNIED BROTHERS HOUSE OF BATIK

One of many good batik shops on Arab Street, Aljunied Brothers also carries ready-made dresses, sarongs, tablecloths, shirts, stuffed toys and the like in batik.

➕ F5 ✉ 91 & 95 Arab Street ☎ 6293 2751 ⏱ Mon–Sat 10–6. Closed Fri 12.30–2 🚇 Bugis

BATIK EMPORIUM

Leather, briefcases, camera cases and purses as well as batik shirts, dresses and sarongs.

➕ F6 ✉ 138 Arab Street ☎ 6297 2955 ⏱ Mon–Sat 10–7.30, Sun 12–6.30 🚇 Bugis

EASTERN CARPETS

Walls and floors are covered with old and new Persian and Pakistani carpets, both hand-woven and mass-produced.

➕ F6 ✉ #03-26/7 Raffles City Shopping Centre, 252 North Bridge Road ☎ 6338 8135 ⏱ Daily 10.30–9.30 🚇 City Hall

HOLLAND ROAD SHOPPING CENTRE

Ethnic goods from all over Asia. Includes porcelain, cloisonné, arts and crafts and clothing.

➕ Off map to west ✉ 211 Holland Avenue ☎ 6338 8135 ⏱ Daily 10–9 🚌 5, 7, 61, 106

INDIAN BAZAAR

In Indian bazaar fashion, this shop is bursting with textile, mats, saris, posters, craftworks and furniture.

➕ E7 ✉ #07-09 High Street Plaza, 77 High Street ☎ 6336 6242 ⏱ Daily 10–9 🚇 City Hall

MALAY VILLAGE

Located in the heart of Geylang, this collection of Malay buildings showcases local talent and houses an interesting collection of objects.

➕ K4 ✉ 39 Geylang Serai ☎ 6748 4700 ⏱ Daily 10–10 🚇 Paya Lebar

POPPY FABRIC

All the colors of the rainbow are represented in the lovely Thai and Chinese silks in this store and others specializing in textiles along fascinating Arab Street.

➕ F5 ✉ 111 Arab Street ☎ 6296 6352 ⏱ Mon–Sat 10–6.15 🚇 Bugis

SELECT BOOK SHOP

This cosy bookshop carries Singapore's largest selection of books on Southeast Asia, with an extensive range of academic texts, travel guides and coffee-table books.

➕ B5 ✉ #03-15 Tanglin Shopping Centre, 19 Tanglin Road ☎ 6732 1515 ⏱ Mon–Sat 9.30–6.30 🚇 Orchard

THANDAPANI

This traditional provisions shop specializes in spices used in Indian cooking.

➕ E5 ✉ 124 Dunlop Street ☎ 6292 3163 ⏱ Daily 9–9 🚇 Bugis

CARPET AUCTIONS

Taking in a carpet auction can be a fun way to spend a Sunday. Several carpet companies hold auctions then, usually at the Hyatt, the Hilton or the Holiday Inn. Carpets are spread out for easy viewing from about 10am until just after noon. Estimated market prices are posted and a Continental-type buffet breakfast is often free to participants. Auctions usually start about 1pm. Depending on the number of viewers and the size of their wallets, bidding proceeds at a fast pace. Expect to get 50–70 percent off the estimated price, or at least start the bidding there.

Watches & Jewelry

JADE

The written Chinese character for jade signifies beauty, nobility and purity, and the stone is much valued by the Chinese. The value of jade lies in its color, texture and translucency. The most common types are nephrite and jadeite, both of which are very hard and cold. Nephrite is paler; jadeite is more vivid. And green is not the only color for jade: it comes in many hues, ranging from green to pure white and lavender.

APOLLO GOLDSMITHS

One of many shops that sells gold jewelry along Buffalo Road and Serangoon Road. Gold is sold by the gram, so any difference in cost is due to the design and work.

E5 #01-08, Blk 664 Buffalo Road 6296 1838 Daily 10.30–8.30 Bugis

THE HOUR GLASS

Fine watches from Switzerland, Germany and the United States in all major brands.

C5 6 Scotts Road, #01-10 Scotts 6235 6527 Daily 11–8.45 Orchard

JOSI GEMS

If you're looking for quality loose gems, such as diamonds, emeralds and rubies, this shop is worth a stop.

E6 #08-15 Park Mall, 9 Penang Road 6338 7423 Mon–Fri 11–5, Sat 11–2.30 Dhoby Ghaut

LUCKY PLAZA

Many shops here sell freshwater pearls, including choker and bracelet sets. Many colors are available.

C5 304 Orchard Road 6235 3294 Daily 10–9 Orchard

MIKIMOTO

Cultured pearls in necklaces, rings and earrings are available in this boutique shop inside Takashimaya department store. Black pearl rings are another specialty.

C6 #02-04 Takashimaya, 391 Orchard Road 6735 1184 Daily 10–9.30 Orchard

NASH JEWELRY

This shop and a branch in Tanglin Shopping Centre (➤ 72) sell jewelry retail and wholesale.

C5 #01-28 Orchard Towers, 400 Orchard Road 6735 5328 Mon–Sat 10–7.30, Sun 2–5.30 Orchard

PENG KWEE

Second-hand watch dealers who specialize in brands such as Rolex, Piaget, Patek Philipe and Chopard.

E7 #01-45A Peninsula Plaza, 111 North Bridge Road 6334 0155 Daily 10–8 Orchard

ROLEX

Rolex watches at prices that guarantee they are the real thing.

C5 #02-01 Tong Building, 302 Orchard Road 6737 9033 Mon–Fri 9.15–5.15 Orchard

SINCERE WATCH LIMITED

Another authorized dealer in fine European watches. The salesmen know their stuff and offer good discounts.

F6 8 Temasek Boulevard, 23–03 Suntec Tower Three 6737 4592 Daily 10.30–9 City Hall

TERESE JADE & MINERALS

Jade is a Chinese favorite. Check out the loose beads and stones—you can make your own jewelry or have it custom made on the premises.

B5 #01-28 Tanglin Shopping Centre, 19 Tanglin Road 6734 0379 Mon–Sat 10–6 Orchard

Electrical & Electronic Goods

APPLE CENTRE AT FUNAN

Mac fans can now get the full range of Apple products, including the iPod, at good prices.

⊞ E7 ✉ #05-07 Funan IT Mall, 109 North Bridge Road ☎ 6336 9929 ⏰ Daily 10–8 🚇 City Hall

CATHAY PHOTO STORE

Carries a great range of traditional and digital cameras and accessories. Knowlegeable staff. You can haggle a bit here.

⊞ F7 ✉ #2-219 Marina Square, 6 Raffles Boulevard ☎ 6339 6188 ⏰ Mon–Sat 10.30–8, Sun 10.30–7 🚇 City Hall

CHALLENGER SUPERSTORE

Specializes in computer-related products. Stocks a good range but can be expensive.

⊞ E7 ✉ #06-00 Funan IT Mall, 109 North Bridge Road ☎ 6336 7747 ⏰ Daily 10.30–8 🚇 City Hall

COURTS

Two floors are filled with appliances ranging from washing machines and dryers to clocks, stereos and cameras.

⊞ Off map to northwest ✉ Levels 2 & 3, Plaza Singapura, 68 Orchard Road ☎ 6333 1898 ⏰ Daily 11–10 🚇 Dhoby Ghaut

FUNAN CENTRE

A huge range of computers and accessories, as well as photographic equipment.

⊞ E7 ✉ 109 North Bridge Road ☎ 6336 4235 ⏰ Daily 11–8 🚇 City Hall

HARVEY NORMAN

Specializes in household appliances, TVs and audio equipment. You'll find branches island-wide.

⊞ D6 ✉ #03-08 Centrepoint, 176 Orchard Road ☎ 6732 8686 ⏰ Daily 10.30–9 🚇 Somerset

MOHAMED MUSTAFA & SAMSUDDIN CO

Three floors of a wide range of goods including clothing, CDs, jewelry, small appliances, stereos, luggage, clocks and cameras, usually at lower prices. One of the more popular with the locals.

⊞ H4 ✉ #01/2/3 Serangoon Plaza, 320 Serangoon Road ☎ 6298 2967 ⏰ Mon–Fri 9am–10pm, Sat, Sun 9am–10.30pm 🚌 66, 67

SIM LIM SQUARE

Several floors of shops sell a large variety of electronic goods, including appliances, computers, software, televisions. Look for the red "Merlion" logo that indicates a "Good Retailer" approved by the STB. And beware hasslers!

⊞ E5 ✉ 1 Rochor Canal Road ☎ 6336 3922 ⏰ Daily 10.30am–11pm (individual shops' hours may vary) 🚇 Bugis

TANGS

The third floor of this popular department store has shelf after shelf of cameras, televisions and electronic items.

⊞ C5 ✉ 320 Orchard Road ☎ 6737 5500 ⏰ Mon–Fri 11–9, Sat 11–9.30; Sun 12.30–8 🚇 Orchard

BEFORE LEAVING HOME

Some say some that Singapore no longer carries the best prices on electronics. Before leaving home, check the prices and model numbers of the brands you are interested in so you have a point of comparison when visiting the hundreds of electronics shops here. Most items can be purchased with or without a guarantee; whether you choose to have one may affect the price. Read the guarantee carefully if you do choose one, and make sure the voltage of the item and the wiring and plug fit your requirements at home.

Theater, Music & Cinema

WHERE TO FIND OUT WHAT'S ON

Concerts and theater are very popular, particularly for weekend shows. Details of events, their venues and where to buy tickets can be found in Singapore's daily morning newspaper, the *Straits Times*, and various free publications. Tickets are obtainable from SISTIC and TicketCharge outlets at Centrepoint, Tanglin Mall, Wisma Atria, Great World City, Raffles City Shopping Centre, Takashimaya Store, Funan Centre, Juntion 8 and Bugis Junction. Bookings ☎ 6348 5555 and ☎ 6296 2929.

A NATION OF FILMGOERS

Cinemas pack in film lovers all over the island. A great number of English-language films are shown, as well as some Chinese films, usually with English subtitles. At weekends, it is often necessary to book in advance. Singapore's most luxurious film-viewing, with drinks brought to your seat, costs you about S$22 a ticket, triple the normal S$7.50.

BOOM BOOM BOOM
Drag queens and stand-up comedy are the staples at this local institution. Check media for current shows and reserve early.
✚ ciii; E8 ✉ 130–132 Amoiy Street, Far East Square ☎ 6435 0030 🚇 Tanjong Pagar

CHINESE OPERA
Chinese opera—known as *wayang*—is staged from time to time in theaters, and shows aimed at tourists take place regularly on Clarke Quay (► 40), but the best place to see it is in the street. Professional troupes, often from China, set up makeshift stages all over Singapore, especially during Chinese New Year and the festival of the Hungry Ghosts (► 4).

CINEPLEX ORCHARD
One of Singapore's largest cinemas complexes, it includes a video arcade, shops and a food center.
✚ D6 ✉ 8 Grange Road ☎ 6235 1155 🕐 Ticket sales: daily 10–8 🚇 Somerset

ESPLANADE—THEATRES ON THE BAY (► 39)

INDIAN DANCE
Singapore's Indian population takes its dance very seriously, and local dance academies put on public performances. The exacting steps and hand gestures, the exciting rhythms and the brilliant costumes of dance forms such as *orissi* are an

unusual delight and well worth checking out.
Nrityalaya Aesthetics Society
✚ E6 ✉ 155 Waterloo Street ☎ 6336 6537 🚇 Bugis

Singapore Indian Fine Arts Society
✚ F4 ✉ 2A Starlight Road, off Serangoon Road ☎ 6299 5925 🚌 66, 67

KALLANG THEATRE
This is Singapore's largest theater; it is here that crowd-pulling shows from around the world, such as *Cats*, are staged.
✚ H6 ✉ Stadium Walk ☎ 6345 8488 🚌 16

THE SUBSTATION
Modern, and often local, plays are performed within a small studio theater, along with concerts and other events.
✚ E6 ✉ 45 Armenian Street ☎ 6337 7535 🚇 City Hall

VICTORIA THEATRE AND CONCERT HALL
Classical and other music concerts take place here. Check local media for concert and peformance details.
✚ dI; E7 ✉ 11 Empress Place ☎ 6339 6120 🚇 Raffles Place

YONG SIEW CONSERVATORY OF MUSIC
Based at the National University of Singapore this premier institution offers a concert and recital program open to the public.
✚ Off map to west ✉ University Cultural Centre Hall ☎ 6874 1167 🚇 Buona Vista MRT, then bus 95, 96

Sports & Leisure

BUONA VISTA SWIMMING COMPLEX

Handy for those staying in the Holland Village area, this complex includes a competition pool as well as teaching and wading pools.

⊞ Off map to west ⊠ 76 Holland Drive ☎ 6778 0244 ⏱ Daily 10–10 🚇 Buona Vista

CLEMENTI SWIMMING CLUB

This club has teaching, wading and competition pools.

⊞ Off map to west ⊠ 520 Clementi Avenue ☎ 6779 0577 ⏱ Daily 8am–9.30pm 🚇 Clementi

FARRER PARK TENNIS CENTRE

A short taxi ride to the north of Orchard Road, this 8-court complex is near a swimming pool. Reserve ahead.

⊞ E4 ⊠ 1 Rutland Road ☎ 6299 4166 ⏱ Daily 7am–10pm

KALLANG NETBALL CENTRE

This modern facility is in the grounds of the National Stadium. There are 6 courts here but you should call ahead.

⊞ H5 ⊠ 52 Stadium Road ☎ 6348 1291 ⏱ Daily 7am–10pm 🚇 Kallang

NATIONAL STADIUM

Check papers for details of major sporting events.

⊞ H5 ⊠ Stadium Road ☎ 6348 1291 🚇 Kallang

RIVER VALLEY SWIMMING COMPLEX

A near-city location makes this dual pool complex popular with visitors serious about swimming. An adjacent teaching pool is available.

⊞ E7 ⊠ 1 River Valley Road ☎ 6337 6275 ⏱ Daily 8am–9.30pm 🚇 City Hall

TAMPINES STADIUM ROCK CLIMBING WALL

This excellent wall is one of the few in Singapore.

⊞ Off map to east ⊠ 25 Tampines Street ☎ 6781 1980 ⏱ Daily 7am–10pm 🚇 Tampines

TANGLIN GOLF COURSE

Handy to Orchard Road and opposite the southern entrance to the Botanic Gardens, this 5-hole golf course is the perfect place to practise your strokes.

⊞ A5 ⊠ 130E Harding Road ☎ 6473 7236 ⏱ Daily 7am–7.30pm 🚌 7, 106, 123, 174

TANGLIN TENNIS CENTRE

There are 4 courts at this popular facility, a short bus ride from Orchard Road, next to the compact Tanglin Golf Course. Book ahead.

⊞ A5 ⊠ 130E Harding Road ☎ 6473 7236 ⏱ Daily 7am–10pm 🚌 7, 106, 123, 174

TOA PAYOH PÉTANQUE COURTS

The main centre for this Gallic pastime, with 8 specialist *pétanque* courts.

⊞ E2 ⊠ 297A Lorong 6, Toa Payoh ☎ 6259 2916 ⏱ Daily 7am–10pm 🚇 Toa Payoh

SOCCER ETCETERA

Singaporeans love to watch soccer on television, especially European competitions, although Singapore's own league has a fair local following. If there is one sport that's exclusive in the island state, it would have to be golf. It's as much an excuse to carry on business outdoors as a chance for exercise, and in the pursuit of that elusive deal, golfers stride the fairways of some of the world's most rarefied clubs. Outsiders are welcome at most, however, and they're a good place to meet the friendly locals. Tennis is also another popular sport, despite the humid equatorial climate. To keep fit and get cool at the same time swimming is tops.

Bars

ONE FOR THE ROAD

After working a 10- to 12-hour day, your average Singaporean either heads home to relax with family members; while those who are young and single most likely stop at a favorite bar for a drink en route. Weekends see increased nightlife activity; clubs do a roaring trade and attract expats and locals alike, especially those in the courting mode. As in other large cities, there is a good selection of Irish pubs and October brings a quota of German-inspired beer fests. And don't leave Singapore without having a gin sling at the famous Long Bar at Raffles Hotel (➤ 26, 55).

CARNEGIE'S

This lively bar, with its emphasis on rock music and occasional bar-top dancing, is favored by locals and expatriates alike.

✚ ciii; E8 ✉ 44–45 Pekin Street, Far East Square ☎ 6534 0850 ⏰ Tue–Fri 11am–2am, Sat 5pm–3am, Sun 5pm–midnight 🚇 Raffles Place

CHANGI SAILING CLUB

Although a private club and a long way out of town, this makes a lovely, relaxing place for an evening drink and meal, which can be taken on the small balcony overlooking the beach, under the palm trees or in the comfortable bar. Non-members are admitted for a dollar Monday to Friday evenings.

✚ Off map to northeast ✉ 32 Netheravon Road ☎ 6545 2876 🍴 Restaurant: daily 10–10 🚇 MRT to Tampines then bus 29

THE DUBLINER IRISH PUB

Set in a former colonial mansion this popular pub, with its plush interior, serves excellent food, too.

✚ D6 ✉ 165 Penang Road ☎ 6735 2220 ⏰ Daily noon–2am 🚇 Dhoby Ghaut

ICE COLD BEER

A noisy, hectic, happening place where the beers are kept on ice under the glass-topped bar.

✚ D6 ✉ 9 Emerald Hill ☎ 6735 9929 ⏰ Mon–Fri 5pm–2am, Sat, Sun 5pm–3am 🚇 Somerset

THE LONG BAR BAR & BILLARDS ROOM

The Singapore Sling is usually high on a visitor's list of things to taste in Singapore, and the place to savor it is undoubtedly the Bar and Billiards Room and the Long Bar, both in the Raffles Hotel (➤ 26, 55), where the drink was first served.

✚ F6 ✉ Raffles Hotel Arcade ☎ 6337 1886 ⏰ Sun–Thu 11am–1am, Fri, Sat 6pm–2am 🚇 City Hall

NEXT PAGE PUB

Next door to the more hip Front Page this trendy shophouse, decked out in the Chinese style, is popular with expats and there's a pool table.

✚ D7 ✉ 17 Mohamed Sultan Road ☎ 6835 1693 ⏰ Daily 2pm–3am 🚌 32, 54, 195

PAULANER BRAHAUS

Offers authentic Bavarian cuisine and the popular, freshly-brewed Munich beer in a range of types. The rustic setting is reminiscent of German microbreweries.

✚ F7 ✉ 9 Raffles Boulevard, #01-01 Times Square ☎ 6883 2572 ⏰ Sun–Thu 11.30am–1am, Fri–Sat 11.30am–2am 🚌 32, 54, 195 🚇 City Hall

POST BAR

Part of the stylish Fullerton hotel (➤ 84), this bar serves a selection of classic and fruity cocktails.

✚ di; F7 ✉ 1 Fullerton Square ☎ 6877 8135 ⏰ Mon–Fri noon–2am, Sat, Sun 5pm–2am 🚇 Raffles Place

Nightclubs

BAR NONE
Located in the bsement of the Marriot Hotel. Resident bands play rock from the 1970s to the present on high-quality sound systems.
✚ C5 ✉ 320 Orchard Road ☎ 6831 4657 🕒 Mon 7pm–2am, Tue–Fri, Sun 7pm–3am, Sat 7pm–4am 🚇 Orchard

CLUB EDEN
A hip crowd gathers in this club modelled on an underground club in New York for dancing along to the house DJ's garage and dance music. The bar pours specialty drinks such as Citrus Sins, Adam's Apples and Serpent's Bites. Dress is smart casual.
✚ D7 ✉ 25 Mohamed Sultan Road ☎ 6738 0720 🕒 Daily 6pm–3am 🚌 14, 32, 54

EUROPA MUSIC UNDERGROUND
With its prime Orchard Road location, nightly live bands (except Mondays) and smart, young crowd, this place was a hit from day one. Retro music and good dance area.
✚ D6 ✉ 360 Orchard Road ☎ 6235 3301 🕒 Daily 6pm–3am 🚇 Somerset

HARRY'S QUAYSIDE
A riverside location close to the city makes this one of Singapore's most popular places for a drink, and the crowd often spills out onto the pavement. Blues on Sundays, jazz Wednesday to Saturday.
✚ dl; E7 ✉ 28 Boat Quay ☎ 6538 3029 🕒 Mon–Thu

11am–midnight; Fri, Sat 11am–3am, Sun 11am–1am 🚌 16, 31, 55

LOX
Soul, R & B and hip hop are the house style at this popular place for the young dance crowd.
✚ E7 ✉ Block 3C, River Valley Road, #02-04 Clarke Quay ☎ 6334 4942 🕒 Daily 7pm–3am 🚇 Clarke Quay

PALONG LOBBY BAR
Located in the Rendezvous Hotel, you get great cocktails in tranquil surroundings.
✚ C5 ✉ 9 Bras Basah Road ☎ 6335 1880 🕒 Mon–Thu 3pm–11pm, Fri, Sat 3pm–1am, Sun 3pm–midnight 🚇 Dhoby Ghaut

PAPA JOE'S
This vibrant nightspot, with a great Orchard Road location, is popular with locals and expats alike. Tex-Mex food with a Mediterranean twist and the mango margaritas are legendary. Great pizzas.
✚ D6 ✉ 180 Orchard Road ☎ 6732 7012 🕒 Daily 5pm–3am 🚇 Somerset

ZOUK
Founded in 1990, this is Singapore's most famous club—with good reason. Excellent in-house and guest DJs spin the discs nightly. It's is in a converted godown near the River View Hotel, next to two other good clubs, Phuture and Velvet Underground, all three expensive.
✚ C7 ✉ 17–21 Jiak Kim Street ☎ 6738 2988 🕒 Daily 7pm–3am 🚌 16

DANCE CLUBS

Like elsewhere, Singapore dance clubs tend to suit particular groups of revelers. While expats can be found at such places as Harry's Quayside and Papa Joe's. the mostly young locals find Europa Music Underground and Lox suit their tastes (for details of these clubs see this page left). Cover charges range from S$12 to S$25 and usually include one drink.

Luxury Hotels

PRICES

Expect to pay the following prices per person per night:

Luxury   over S$200
Mid-range S$100–S$200
Budget   under S$100

TOP OF THE RANGE

One of Singapore's newest and most elegant hotels, the Ritz-Carlton Millenia (➕ F7 ✉ 7 Raffles Avenue ☎ 6337 8888; www.ritzcarlton.com 🚇 City Hall), provides all you can imagine in luxury and comfort. With its sumptuously appointed rooms, excellent restaurants, large pool and extensive business facilities, it's ideal for buisness travelers and for visitors who can afford to splurge. A commanding position on Marina Bay provides fantastic views over the harbor and the new Esplanade theater complex.

Singapore's most recent luxury offering, the Fullerton (➕ di; F7 ✉ 1 Fullerton Square ☎ 6735 8388; www. fullertonhotel.com 🚇 Raffles Place) is located in the heritage GPO building and has lovely river views.

FOUR SEASONS

Ideally located just behind Orchard Road with top-notch facilities, two pools, air-conditioned tennis courts and good restaurants.
➕ C5 ✉ 190 Orchard Boulevard ☎ 6734 1110; www.fourseasons.com/singapore 🚇 Orchard

GOODWOOD PARK

Formerly the Teutonia Club for German expatriates, this hotel retains its charm. It is well located, close to Orchard Road, and has lovely gardens.
➕ C5 ✉ 22 Scotts Road ☎ 6737 7411; www.goodwood parkhotel.com.sg 🚇 Orchard

MARINA MANDARIN

With a superb waterfront location in the Marina Bay, this 575-room luxury hotel offers the ultimate in facilities, including a host of recreation possibilities.
➕ F7 ✉ 6 Raffles Boulevard ☎ 6845 1000; fax 6845 1199 🚇 City Hall

MARRIOTT

This Singapore landmark, formerly the Dynasty, retains its original distinctive pagoda-style roof and features a roof-top pool and business and fitness facilities. Central location above Tangs store.
➕ C5 ✉ 320 Orchard Road ☎ 6735 8967; www.marriott.com 🚇 Orchard

ORIENTAL

The 21-story Oriental is one of three luxury hotels built on reclaimed land overlooking Marina Bay. It is conveniently close to Marina Square shopping mall—good for last-minute gifts—and Suntec City, which incorporates one of the largest conference and exhibition halls in Asia and is Singapore's newest central business district.
➕ F7 ✉ 5 Raffles Avenue, Marina Square ☎ 6338 0066; www.mandarin-oriental.com/singapore 🚇 City Hall

RAFFLES

To relive the golden age of travel, stay at Raffles (► 26), Singapore's most famous hotel, first opened in 1887. All the accommodations are suites and are expensive.
➕ F6 ✉ 1 Beach Road ☎ 6337 1886; www.raffles.com 🚇 City Hall

SHANGRI-LA

One of Singapore's finest hotels, with all the facilities you'd expect, plus magnificent gardens and a golf putting green. Good food and service.
➕ B5 ✉ 22 Orange Grove Road ☎ 6737 3644; www.shangri-la.com 🚇 Orchard

SWISSÔTEL THE STAMFORD

Reputedly the tallest hotel in the world outside the United States, this luxury hotel has every possible amenity, including 16 restaurants, a business center, sports facilities and views.
➕ F7 ✉ 2 Stamford Road ☎ 6338 8585; www.swissotel.com 🚇 City Hall

Mid-Range Hotels

ALBERT COURT HOTEL
An eight-story hotel comprising 136 rooms in a renovated shophouse near Little India with café and good facilities.
✚ E5 ✉ 180 Albert Street ☎ 6339 3939; www.albertcourt.sg 🚇 Bugis

BERJAYA DUXTON HOTEL
This classy hotel is a converted shophouse. It has one of the best French restaurants in town, which supplies excellent breakfasts (included in the room price) and dinners.
✚ D8 ✉ 83 Duxton Road ☎ 6227 7678; www.berjaya resorts.com.sg 🚇 Tanjong Pagar

EXCELSIOR HOTEL
Very well located, with Chinatown, the colonial Civic District, Boat Quay, Clarke Quay and Marina Bay all a stone's throw away. Swimming pool.
✚ E5 ✉ 3–5 Coleman Street ☎ 6337 2200; fax 6339 3847 🚇 City Hall

GARDEN HOTEL
This pleasant hotel is slightly off the beaten track, but represents very good value, with the facilities of a much fancier place, including a pool. Within walking distance of Orchard and Scotts roads.
✚ C4 ✉ 14 Balmoral Road ☎ 6235 3344; fax 6235 9730 🚇 Newton

INN AT TEMPLE STREET
Right in the heart of Chinatown, this charming hotel has traditional Peranakan furniture in the lobby and guest rooms. Its café serves Western and Asian dishes.
✚ bll; D8 ✉ 36 Temple Street, Chinatown ☎ 6221 5333; www.theinn.com.sg 🚌 84, 166, 197

ROYAL
One of Singapore's older hotels with spacious rooms at very good rates. A five-minute walk from Novena MRT and, in the other direction, the famous Newton Circus hawker center. Swimming pool.
✚ D4 ✉ 36 Newton Road ☎ 6253 4411; fax 6235 8668 🚇 Novena MRT

ROYAL PEACOCK HOTEL
Nestled in a row of converted shophouses in Chinatown's relatively low-key, red-light district, the Royal Peacock is awash with European furniture and deep carpets, and bed linens are plum and emerald green.
✚ D8 ✉ 55 Keong Saik Road ☎ 6324 6905; www.royalpeaockhotel.com 🚇 Outram Park

TRADERS HOTEL
This is near the Botanic Gardens and Orchard Road. Family apartments have small kitchens and rooms with foldaway beds that double as meeting rooms for business travelers.
✚ B5 ✉ 1A Cuscaden Road ☎ 6738 2222; fax 6831 4314 🚇 Orchard

SINGAPORE'S ONLY URBAN RESORT
Swissôtel Merchant Court Hotel (✚ cl; E7 ✉ 20 Merchant Road ☎ 6337 2288; www.swissotel.com 🚇 City Hall), on the Singapore River between Clarke Quay and Chinatown, is always a good choice. The extensive facilities include a great pool, a business center, self-service laundry facilities and a relaxing lobby bar, known as Crossroads.

Budget Accommodations

HOSTELS AND CHEAP STAYS

Singapore, unlike many Asian cities, does not have a plethora of good, cheap accommodations. Some of the places on this page charge around S$100 per night per room, and are of a good standard. There are cheaper establishments, especially around Bencoolen Street, and some dormitory-style hostels, known as "crash pads," but the standards of cleanliness and privacy can be quite low. The STB booklet entitled *Budget Hotels* lists a number of places that charge less than S$60 per night.

BEN COOLEN

This 74-room budget hotel is near the Singapore Art Museum and Little India and not far from Orchard Road and the Marina area.

➕ E6 ✉ 47 Bencoolen Street ☎ 6336 0822; www.hotel bencoolen.com Ⓜ Dhoby Ghaut

BROADWAY

A Serangoon Road location puts this hotel in the middle of the Little India district. Standards are high and the staff friendly. Good Indian restaurant next door.

➕ E5 ✉ 195 Serangoon Road ☎ 6292 4661; fax 6291 6414 Ⓜ Bugis

DAMENLOU

In Chinatown. Rooms are clean, with en-suite facilities. Restaurant and rooftop terrace.

➕ dll; E8 ✉ 12 Ann Siang Hill ☎ 6221 1900; fax 6225 8500 Ⓜ Outram Park

LITTLE INDIA GUEST HOUSE

Facilities are basic—all rooms share a bathroom and there's no café or bar—but the location is right in the heart of Little India. Good if your budget is limited.

➕ E5 ✉ 3 Veerasamy Road ☎ 6294 2866; fax 6298 4866 Ⓜ Bugis

MAJESTIC

Refurbishment has stripped this classic backpackers' retreat of its charm, but the good facilities, warm welcome and great location on the edge of Chinatown compensate.

➕ all; D8 ✉ 31–7 Bukit Pasoh Road ☎ 6222 3377; www.majestic-singapore.com Ⓜ Outram Park

METROPOLE

This hotel, across the street from Raffles, is a cut above basic. The famed Imperial Herbal Restaurant (➤ 64) is here.

➕ F6 ✉ 41 Seah Street ☎ 6336 3611; fax 6339 3610 Ⓜ City Hall

METROPOLITAN YMCA

One of a number of YMCAs in Singapore, with a swimming pool. Book ahead.

➕ B4 ✉ 60 Stevens Road ☎ 6737 7755; www.mymca. org.sg Ⓜ MRT to Orchard then bus 196, 190, 132, 105, 605

NEW 7TH STOREY HOTEL

Close to Burgis MRT, this hostel/hotel offers air-conditioned rooms and dormitories.

➕ F6 ✉ 229 Rocher Road ☎ 6737 0251; fax 6334 3550 Ⓜ Bugis

STRAND

A budget hotel with café and en-suite bathrooms.

➕ E6 ✉ 25 Bencoolen Street ☎ 6338 1866; www.strand hotel.com.sg Ⓜ Dhoby Ghaut

YMCA INTERNATIONAL HOUSE

This YMCA, with a prime location near the start of Orchard Road, has a fitness center, pool and a McDonalds is in the building. Reserve well in advance.

➕ E6 ✉ 1 Orchard Road ☎ 6336 6000; www.mymca. org.sg Ⓜ Dhoby Ghaut

SINGAPORE
travel facts

ESSENTIAL FACTS

Backpackers
- Accommodation is generally expensive, with inexpensive options fairly hard to find, although budget-priced hostels offer rooms from as little as S$20–S$40 per night (► 86).
- Food is inexpensive compared with prices in Europe and the US. A meal at a hawker center may cost as little as S$3.

Car rental
- Car rental is expensive and public transportation is very good.
- If you do decide to rent a car, remember that it is very expensive to take it into Malaysia; it's much better to rent one there. An area day license has to be bought to take a car into the central business district during the week and until mid-afternoon on Saturdays.
- Display coupons in your windscreen in parking lots and designated parking places. Area day licenses and books of coupons can be purchased at newsagents and garages. Steep fines are incurred for failing to display licenses and coupons.
- Driving is on the left. A valid international or other recognized driving license is required.
- Insurance is included in rental fees.

Complaints
- If you wish to complain about the service you have received you can contact the Singapore Tourist Board (► 90) or the Complaints Hotline (☎ 800 736 3366).

Customs regulations
- One liter each of duty-free spirits, wine and beer can be brought into Singapore, along with a reasonable amount of personal items and gifts.
- Duty has to be paid on cigarettes, cigars and tobacco.
- A number of items are prohibited including weapons, firecrackers, drugs, pornographic and pirated material and certain publications. Video cassettes are subject to inspection, for which a fee may be charged.
- There is no limit to the amount of currency you may bring in.
- For customs inquiries: ☎ 6736 6622 (Terminal 1) ☎ 6736 6622 (Terminal 2)

Departure tax
- A departure tax of S$15 and passenger security service charge of S$6 are included in the cost of your air ticket.

Electricity
- Singapore operates on 220–240 volts and most sockets take British-style three-pin plugs.
- Most hotels supply adaptors.

Etiquette
- Singapore is very regulated with laws against jaywalking, spitting and littering, among other things. Fines for littering can be about S$1,000, as they can be for smoking in the wrong place.
- Smoking is prohibited on public transportation, in elevators, government offices, theaters, air-conditioned restaurants and shopping malls.
- Tipping is discouraged in restaurants, hotels or taxis, though restaurants charge for service (a sales tax and an entertainment tax, which amounts to a total of around 15 percent, often expressed on bills and receipts as "+++").

- Casual clothes are acceptable in most places, though some clubs and bars stipulate no shorts and sandals. Men and women should cover arms and legs when visiting all temples.
- In temples, mosques and other places of worship, be respectful: don't make too much noise and, in Muslim and Hindu places of worship, remove your footwear before entering.
- Most Asians consider it rude to point with your finger; use your whole hand instead.
- When dining with Muslims and Hindus, do not eat with your left hand (considered unclean); although they often use cutlery. Be aware that Muslims do not eat pork and many Hindus do not eat beef or are vegetarian. Muslims do not eat and drink in daylight hours during Ramadan, the fasting month.
- Chopsticks are the norm in Chinese restaurants, though spoons and forks are available.
- Eating is a national pastime, especially for the Chinese, so don't be surprised if hardly a word is uttered once the food is served. All concentration is devoted to the matter at hand – eating!
- If you are invited to someone's home at Chinese New Year, the gift to take is oranges and never an odd number, which the Chinese consider unlucky.

Goods and services tax (GST)

- If you buy goods costing S$300 or more, you may, as a visitor, be eligible to claim back the 5 percent GST.
- Obtain a Global Refund Cheque (check) from the shop. Make sure you have your passport whenever you go shopping if you are planning to claim this tax back.

- On departure from Singapore you need to produce your copy of this form, along with the goods themselves, at special counters at the airport in order to obtain your GST rebate. Allow at least 15 minutes. Inquiries ☎ 6225 6238

Lavatories

- There are easily accessible, clean restrooms in almost every shopping and hawker center.
- MRT stations usually have toilets.
- It is acceptable to use toilets in hotels, even if not a guest.
- Some facilities charge 10 or 20 cents and will then provide toilet paper.
- Be prepared to use squatting toilets occasionally, though you will find most places offer a choice.

Money matters

- You can change money at the airport on arrival, or at hotels, banks and money-changers, who can be found all over town (and whose rate is slightly better than that given by banks and hotels). Most major banks are in the Central Business District (CBD).
- Automatic teller machines (ATMs) are everywhere.
- Many shops, restaurants and hotels take credit cards.

Opening hours

- Stores: usually Mon to Sat 10 to 9.30; some close earlier and others keep longer hours. Most shops are open on Sunday.
- Banks: Mon to Fri 9 to 3; Sat 10 to 12.
- Offices: usually Mon to Fri 9 to 5; some open for half a day on Saturdays and others open earlier and close later.
- Doctors' clinics: Mon to Fri 9 to 6; Sat 9 to 12.

Places of worship

- Anglican: St. Andrew's Cathedral
  ✉ St. Andrew's Road ☎ 6337 6104
- Jewish Orthodox: Synagogue
  ✉ Waterloo Street ☎ 6336 0692
- Methodist: Wesley Methodist
  Church ✉ 5 Fort Canning Road ☎ 6336
  1433
- Roman Catholic: Cathedral of the
  Good Shepherd ✉ Queen Street
  ☎ 6337 2036
- Muslim mosques and Hindu
  temples are listed in the Top 25
  Sights (► 25–50) and Singapore's
  Best (► 51–62).

Public holidays

- New Year's Day: 1 January
  Hari Raya Puasa: one day,
  January/February
  Chinese New Year: two days,
  February
  Good Friday: March/April
  Hari Raya Haji: one day, April
  Labour Day: 1 May
  Vesak Day: one day, May
  National Day: 9 August
  Diwali: November
  Christmas Day: 25 December

Safety and comfort

- Singapore is probably the safest
  Asian country in which to travel,
  with low crime rates making it a
  good destination for women and
  lone travelers to visit.
- Be sure to drink plenty of water
  to avoid heat exhaustion.
- It is safe to drink tap water and to
  eat from foodstalls and hawkers.

Singapore Tourist Board

- Predictably, the ultra-efficient
  Singapore Tourist Board produces
  plenty of free literature about the
  island and tours. Individual guides
  can be hired for specialist needs
  and free sightseeing tours are
  available for transit passengers;

contact the Changi Airport lounge
on arrival. The board's main office
is centrally located in Orchard
Spring Lane off Cuscaden Road
(✉ Tourism Court, 1 Orchard Spring Lane ☎ 6736
6622 ⏰ Mon–Fri 8.30–5, Sat 8.30–1).
Information also from its office in
Raffles Hotel Arcade (✉ #02-34
Raffles Hotel Arcade ☎ 1800 736 2000
⏰ 8.30–7).

- Overseas tourist offices are at:
  Australia ✉ Level 11, AWA Building, 47 York
  Street, Sydney, NSW 2000 ☎ 02 9290 2882/8;
  fax 02 9290 2555
  UK ✉ Carrington House, 126–30 Regent Street,
  London W1B 5JX ☎ 020 7437 0033; fax 020
  7734 2191
  USA ✉ 1156 Avenue of the Americas, Suite 702,
  New York, NY 10036 ☎ 212/302-4861; fax
  212/302-4801 and ✉ 4929 Wilshire Boulevard,
  Suite 510, Beverly Hills, CA 90010 ☎ 323/677-
  0808; fax 323 677-0801
- Many hotels display an extensive
  range of tourist brochures and
  have tour desks with helpful staff
  who can offer ideas on interesting
  things to do during your stay.

GETTING AROUND

Bus

- Buses take exact change, though
  you can always give a dollar coin
  for a journey you know costs less.
- Bus service is numerous and
  frequent. Buy individual tickets
  on the bus (exact change only), or
  use the Transitlink Farecard.
- Machines at the front of the bus
  take the card; press a button for
  the price of your particular
  journey. If you're not sure of the
  amount, ask the driver.
- Singapore Explorer stored-value
  cards are available for use on
  buses—S$14.90 for one day
  (includes a Singapore River tour).
  These cards can be purchased at
  MRT stations and hotels.

- A comprehensive bus and MRT timetable, called the *Transitlink Guide*, can be purchased at newsagents for S$1.50.
- Singapore Bus Service runs a hotline ☎ Mon–Fri 8–5.30, Sat 8–1. Tell them where you are and where you want to go. The number is ☎ 1800 287 2727

MRT

- There are three main mass rapid transit (MRT) lines, running north–south and east–west . The North-East Line opened in 2003.
- Trains run between 5.30am and 12.30am.
- You can buy single tickets, or use the S$7 tourist souvenir stored-value cards for a number of journeys.
- The E3-link card, also a stored-value card (minimum value S$15 plus S$5 deposit), can be used on buses as well as the MRT.
- Tickets can be purchased from machines and from ticket offices. Insert them into machines at the barriers when entering and leaving stations. Take the card with you when you are through the barrier, unless it is a single-journey ticket, in which case the machine will retain the ticket at the end of your journey.
- At the end of your stay refunds can be obtained on any amount outstanding on stored-value cards.
- Useful numbers: MRT ☎ 1800 336 8900; MRT and bus integration ☎ 1800 336 8900

Taxi

- Taxis are easily found on Singapore's roads, though they can be more difficult to come by during rush hours (8am to 9am and 5pm to 7pm), just before midnight, and when it's raining.
- Shopping centers, hotels, sights and stations usually have taxi stands, and apart from these, taxis can also be hailed along the road. A taxi displaying a light at night is for hire.
- Taxis are air-conditioned and comfortable.
- Taxis charge a flat rate of S$2.40. There are surcharges for taxis hired from the airport, for fares between midnight and 6am, for bookings made in advance, and for journeys via the business district or on motorways where electronic road-pricing schemes are operating.
- Taxi drivers sometimes may not have sufficient change to accept large notes (S$50 or higher), so carry some low value notes.
- Reserve in advance for important journeys, such as to the airport. Some taxi companies:
Comfort ☎ 6552 1111/2828
Citycab ☎ 6552 2222
Tibs ☎ 6555 8888

Trishaw

- Singapore's bicycle trishaws are disappearing fast, but this traditional method of transport is popular with tourists around the middle of town. Agree on a price in advance. For tours by trishaw (► 20).

MEDIA & COMMUNICATIONS

Newspapers & magazines

- The main English-language dailies are the *Straits Times*, the *Business Times* and the *New Paper*. The latter is of a tabloid nature, seen as a fun alternative to others and as a result contains very little real news.
- The *International Herald Tribune* is also available, as is a wide range of

91

local and international magazines and publications.

- All publications are subject to strict government-controlled censorship; some foreign magazines and newspapers may be banned for periods of time if articles in them fall foul of the censorship rules.

Post offices

- Post office hours do vary, but the post office at 1 Killiney Road is open Mon–Sat 9–9; Sun 9–4.30.
- Buy stamps in small shops and hotel lobbies as well as at post offices.
- Postcards and airmail letters to all destinations cost 50 cents. Standard letter rate to EuropeUSA is S$1. Prepaid postcards and airmail letters are available.
- General delivery (poste restante) facilities are available at the post office at 🖂 10 Eunos Road ☎ 6741 8857. Simply address mail "Poste Restante, Singapore."

Radio

- There are a number of local radio stations (e.g. FM 90.5, FM98.7, FM95) that play popular music.
- BBC World Service can be picked up on FM88.9.
- News and information in English FM93.8.
- Classical music can be heard on FM92.4.

Telephones

- Phone calls within Singapore are very cheap—local calls cost as little as 10 cents for three-minute blocks.
- Both coin- and card-operated telephones are easy to find. Most restaurants and coffee shops, as well as most shops and sights,

have public phones. They can also be found at MRT stations.
- Comcentre II (🖂 31 Exeter Road ☎ 6734 9465 🕙 24 hours) offers private telephone and fax booths for local and international calls, charging the official rates.
- Phone cards can be purchased at stores and post offices.
- Calls from some hotels are subject to a 20 percent surcharge.
- International calls need to be prefixed by 001, followed by the country code. To call Singapore from outside use country code 65.
- Calls to Malaysia from Singapore need to be prefixed by 020, followed by the area code (Kuala Lumpur–3, Johor–7, Penang–4).
- Operator to call for Singapore numbers ☎ 100; international numbers ☎ 104

Television

- There are five free-to-air Singapore TV channel—you can find programs in English on Channel 5, Channel 8, Channel NewsAsia, Central and Sportcit—and most TV sets can also receive programs broadcast by Malaysia's TV1 and TV2 channels; some may pick up broadcasts from Indonesia. Cable television is widely available, especially on the HDB estates, and broadcasts HBO, Discovery, BBC World, CNN and Star Sports among others. Most hotels offer some cable programing, especially news and movies.

EMERGENCIES

Emergency numbers
- Police ☎ 999
- Fire ☎ 995
- Ambulance ☎ 995

Embassies & consulates

- Australia ✉ 25 Napier Road ☎ 6836 4100 🕐 Mon–Fri 8.30–12.30 and 1.30–4.30
- Canada ✉ 80 Anson Road, #14-00 IBM Towers ☎ 6325 3200 🕐 Mon–Fri 8–12, 2–4
- India ✉ 31 Grange Road ☎ 6737 6777 🕐 Mon–Fri 9–11.30am
- Indonesia ✉ 7 Chatsworth Road ☎ 6737 7422 🕐 Mon–Fri 9–4
- Ireland ✉ 541 Orchard Road, #08-00 Liat Towers ☎ 6238 7616 🕐 9.30–12.30, 2.30–4
- Malaysia ✉ 301 Jervois Road ☎ 6235 0111 🕐 Mon–Fri 8.30–3.30
- New Zealand ✉ 391A Orchard Road, #15-06 Ngee Ann City Tower A ☎ 6235 9966 🕐 Mon–Fri 8.30–4.30
- UK ✉ 325 Tanglin Road ☎ 6473 9333 🕐 Mon–Fri 8.30–5
- USA ✉ 27 Napier Road ☎ 6476 9100 🕐 Mon–Fri 8.30–5.15

Lost property

- Police ☎ 999. Call only after checking thoroughly that the item is missing.
- For lost credit cards:
  American Express ☎ 1800 737 8188
  Diners Card ☎ 6294 4222
  MasterCard ☎ 1800 110 0113
  VISA ☎ 1800 110 0344

Medical treatment

- Singapore's medical system is good by any standards. It offers a mixture of public and private treatment options. Costs—even for hospitalisation—are reasonable by Western standards, although expensive in comparison with other Southeast Asian countries. Make sure you have insurance cover.
- Many hotels offer guests a doctor-on-call service or can recommend a local doctor or clinic for you.
- You can usually just walk into a doctor's surgery or clinic and ask for treatment.
- If you require hospital treatment, you will need to provide proof that you can pay for it.
- The best centrally located hospitals are Mount Elizabeth (☎ 6737 2666) and Gleneagles (☎ 6473 7222). Both have emergency departments.
- Most medicines are available in Singapore. If you have special requirements, either bring enough with you to last for your stay or enquire about their availability before you arrive.

LANGUAGES

- Singapore has four official languages: English, Mandarin, Malay and Tamil. English is widely understood and spoken. A patois know as Singlish is often used. Nominally English, it uses words from other languages, primarily Malay. Its clipped phrases and stresses make interesting listening.
- English-language newspapers, magazines and books are widely available.
- Road signs, bus destinations and tickets all appear in English, and staff in stores, hotels and places of interest speak English.

Index

CityPack
Singapore *Top 25*

ABOUT THE AUTHOR
Vivien Lytton has lived in Singapore and worked in publishing, project-managing illustrated books on Southeast Asia. She maintains a close interest in the region, and in Singapore—one of the world's great crossroads—in particular.

Author *Vivien Lytton* **Edition Reviser** *Rod Ritchie* **Managing Editors** *Apostrophe S Limited*
Cover Design *Tigist Getachew, Fabrizio La Rocca*

A CIP catalogue record for this book is available from the British Library.

ISBN-10: 0 7495 4360 4
ISBN-13: 978 0 7495 4360 0

Published by AA Publishing, a trading name of Automobile Association Developments Limited, whose registered office is Southwood East, Apollo Rise, Farnborough, Hampshire, GU14 0JW. Registered number 1878835.

© **AUTOMOBILE ASSOCIATION DEVELOPMENTS LIMITED 1996, 1999, 2001, 2005**
First published 1996. Revised second edition 1999. Reprinted Apr, Sep, Dec 2000. Revised third edition 2001. Reprinted 2002. Revised fourth edition 2005

Colour separation by Keenes, Andover
Printed and bound by Hang Tai D&P Limited, Hong Kong.

ACKNOWLEDGMENTS
The author would like to thank Debbie Guthrie Haer and Tim Jaycock for their invaluable assistance with this book, and David for his support. Special thanks also to Shamira Bhanu for her help in updating this guide.
The Automobile Association would like to thank the following photographers, libraries and associations for their assistance in the preparation of this book:
Vivien Crump 30; Night Safari 27; Ritz-Carlton Millenia 52; Singapore Esplanade 39t (Photo by Eujin Goh), 39b; Singapore Tourist Board 8/9t, 9r, 11t, 13c, 16cr, 17, 23b, 24cr; Stockbyte 5; Travel Ink/Abbie Enock 46
The remaining pictures are held in the Association's own library (AA WORLD TRAVEL LIBRARY) and were taken by Alex Kouprianoff with the exception of the following:
Ben Davies 61; Nick Hanna Front Cover blurred image (trees), 1t, 2, 4, 6, 8b, 21; Paul Kenward Front Cover performer, Back Cover b, 8/9b, 15cr, 24cl, 54; Ken Paterson Front Cover lantern, temple, buddha, building, food, Back Cover t, cb, 1b, 7tl, 7tc, 8cl, 8ct, 8c, 10c, 11c, 12/13, 13t, 14c, 15cl, 16cl, 16/17, 18c, 19t, 19c, 19cr, 20tr, 20c, 22/23, 22b, 23c, 24c, 25t, 25b, 29b, 31, 32, 36t, 36b, 37t, 37b, 38, 41, 49, 51t, 51b, 55, 59, 63t, 63b, 87t, 87b; Neil Ray 48

A01992	
Fold-out map	© RV Reise- und Verkehrsverlag Munich · Stuttgart
	© Cartography: GeoData
Transport map	© TCS, Aldershot, England